"Reformed"
Is Not Enough

Douglas Wilson, *Reformed Is Not Enough: Recovering the Objectivity of the Covenant*
© 2002 by Douglas Wilson

Published by Canon Press, P.O. Box 8729, Moscow, ID 83843
800-488-2034 / www.canonpress.org
Printed in the United States of America.
Cover design by Paige Atwood

03 04 05 06 07 08 09   9 8 7 6 5 4 3 2

Library of Congress Cataloging-in-Publication Data

Wilson, Douglas, 1953–
   "Reformed" is not enough : recovering the objectivity of the covenant /
   Douglas J. Wilson.
          p. cm.
   Includes bibliographical references.
   ISBN 1-59128-005-2 (pbk.)
   1. Covenant theology. I. Title.
   BT155 .W65 2002
   230'.42—dc21   2002015016

"Reformed"
is Not Enough

Douglas Wilson

CANON PRESS

MOSCOW, IDAHO

Contents

Foreword

On June 22, 2002, Covenant Presbytery of the RPCUS declared that certain teachings at a pastors' conference presented by Steve Schlissel, Steve Wilkins, John Barach and, as the Victorians would have put it, the present writer, involved a "fundamental denial of the essence of the Christian Gospel in the denial of justification by faith alone." Consequently, the four of us were declared to be heretics.

This book project was already well under way when all of this happened and so it cannot be understood as a full-orbed response to the charges. At the same time, given the nature of the subject this book addresses, the material here *can* be considered as part of the provocation and something of a response. The basic theme of this book is what brought about the charges in the first place, and in more than a few passages, I have written responsively with the charges in mind.

The charges assumed (which is incidentally not the same thing as proving) that the positions taken by the speakers were "contrary to the Bible and the Westminster Standards." As a result, in the following pages, there is a closer interaction with the teaching of the Westminster Confession than would otherwise have happened. This was not done in order to "get around" anything in the historic Reformed faith, but rather the reverse. It is our conviction that certain epistemological developments since the Enlightenment have caused many *modern* conservative

Calvinists to read their confessions in a spirit alien to that which produced them. As a result, we were taken to task for denying our confessional heritage at just those places where we were in fact upholding it. This of course does not make us right—as the Westminster theologians themselves told us, and as Steve Schlissel continues to tell us in a loud voice. Something can be "confessional" and wrong. But we are like the obedient boy in the parable—we say the confession *could* be wrong, but then we affirm the confession. Our opponents say the confession is as right as it gets—biblical Christianity in "its purest human expression"—and then proceed to merrily disregard what the confession actually teaches in this area.

What we always want in all "controversies of religion" is a plain and honest resort to Scripture primarily. But when we do this, we are still mindful of our confessional riches and we love that heritage. Given this, it is a bit much to be charged with abandoning our inheritance when those making the charge abandoned the standards long enough ago to give it the color of "a historic position."

No single issue in this collective charge against us is very complicated, but, taken all together, things can become significantly tangled. This is because this was a heresy trial on the cheap—it was a veritable broadside of charges with no apparent need to contact us to get any clarification, no need to document the charges with quotations, no need to distinguish four men with different emphases, and so forth. Simple issues when collectively heaped can still make a big mess.

At the same time, this published response seeks to *name* this imbroglio appropriately. Apart from the specific charges, what exactly is going on here? What worldviews are colliding? This might seem like a nonsensical question to some—"what do you mean *worldviews?*" Both sides of this dispute hold to some variation of postmillennial, Calvinistic, presbyterian, Van Tillian, theonomic, and reformed thought, with additional areas of agreement standing off to the side. I bet none of us voted for Clinton. How could there possibly be enough *material* left over for a fracas?

The answer is found in a contrast we have used many times—medieval versus modern. We believe ourselves to be in the process of recovering what our fathers taught from the Reformation down to the Enlightenment—that is, a Reformed and medieval mindset. We believe our opponents to be sincere and honest Christians, but men who have erroneously made a bad truce with modernity and who have accommodated their theology to the abstract dictates of the Enlightenment. This is why we have been laid on the Procrustean bed of a particular understanding of systematic theology and have had our heretical feet cut off. The irony in this case is that the standards used to judge us were written with the mindset we are returning to and which are drastically misunderstood by the mindset we are rejecting. There will be more on this in the chapters to come.

So the dispute is not imaginary—there are real and important differences between us. We do not believe the differences to constitute heresy—any of the men who have taken this action against us would be welcome to worship at any of our churches and commune with us in the Lord's Supper there. Nevertheless, the differences are real and deep, and the parties that differ ought to be properly named. If it were up to me, building on the acronym TR ("Truly Reformed"), I would suggest that this is a debate between the Enlightenment TRs (ETRs) and the historic reformed. But agreement with this naming will have to wait for further proof.

The basic content of this book appeared originally in a series of sermons preached at Christ Church in Moscow. One of the chapters appeared originally in *The Hammer*, a publication of Community Christian Ministries, while another chapter appeared in *Table Talk*. The rest was written for the occasion.

Douglas Wilson
Christ Church
2002

Part I
Introduction & Bona Fides

1

Judas Was a Christian?

The Church today is in dire need of reformation. This is not said with any denominational exclusivity—the Reformed churches today need reformation as much as anyone else. I say this as one who embraces the richness of the Reformed faith, as will become apparent enough later. But at the same time, *because* of this Reformational commitment, it is still necessary to say that to be Reformed is not enough. We must certainly live up to what we have already attained, but together with this we must not be allowed to assume that the last significant attainment was in the middle of the seventeenth century. *Semper reformanda* is not something we should all chant together right up until someone actually tries it.

One of the great reformational needs in the Church today is the need for us to understand the objectivity of the covenant, and so that is the thrust of this book. Because this covenant is our life, we are called to understand it, embody it, and love the members of it. Not surprisingly, in order to do this, we will have to clear away a good bit of theological debris, which is what I am seeking to do here.

As we undertake the task, one caution should be mentioned at the outset: it is important for us to grasp *all* the issues that will be raised, and this means waiting patiently for some assembly of them later. On a subject of this complexity, the last thing we need is a rush to judgment, which can only result in misunderstanding and confusion. Considerable confusion has already occurred in some quarters, and we need to study the Bible, the theological issues, and our own hearts carefully so that we do not fall into this trap.

With that said we may get right into it. The first question we must consider is this: what is a "Christian" when we use the word in the New Testament sense? Considered from one angle, this question is one of the most important questions a man can ask himself. Tied in with it are all the related questions about God, man, sin, salvation, and revelation. Additionally connected are all the great questions concerning a man's destiny after his course in this life is over.

Given the importance of the question, many may be surprised to learn that the Scriptures say very little about the word *Christian*, which occurs in only three places. And in none of these places is the Word being used in the way we tend to use it. Our application of the Word is certainly a legitimate one, which should be defended and continued, but only if we understand what we are doing.

The first usage in the Bible is a simple reference to what the followers of Christ came to be called—by outsiders. The Scripture tells us that the word *Christian* first came to be applied to the church at Antioch, which consisted of the followers of Christ in that city. "And when he had found him, he brought him unto Antioch. And it came to pass, that a whole year they assembled themselves with the church, and taught much people. And the disciples were called Christians first in Antioch" (Acts 11:26). In this passage, the word is used in the same way other nouns are used— to distinguish one thing from another. Just as we indicate the differences between tables and airplanes by giving them different names, so the pagans of Antioch decided to distinguish the Christians from the Jews and from the many other religious groups that swirled around the empire of that time. No statement was being made about the great questions mentioned above as they might have applied to an individual member of that church. The word was used as a simple noun, as a newspaper writer might have used it.

The second instance is also found in the book of Acts. The apostle Paul was giving an account of himself in front of Festus and Agrippa. As was evident to his judges, his learning was considerable and his presentation of the gospel was serious and affecting. That Festus was stirred can be seen in his outburst, and that Agrippa was unsettled can be seen in his application of the truths of the gospel to himself.

> And as he thus spake for himself, Festus said with a loud voice, Paul, thou art beside thyself; much learning doth make thee mad. But he said, I am not mad, most noble Festus; but speak forth the words of truth and soberness. For the king knoweth of these things, before whom also I speak freely: for I am persuaded that none of these things are hidden from him; for this thing was not done in a corner. King Agrippa, believest thou the prophets? I know that thou believest. Then Agrippa said unto Paul, Almost thou persuadest me to be a Christian. And Paul said, I would to God, that not only thou, but also all that hear me this day, were both almost, and altogether such as I am, except these bonds. (Acts 26:24–29)

In this instance, the context is the presentation of the gospel to those who had not heard or believed it. The apostle wanted them to consider these things, and since the charge had been given to him (along with the other apostles) to preach the gospel to every creature, this is clearly a plea to those in darkness to enter into true light. And obviously, Paul is inviting them to genuine faith, saving belief, and not simply to membership in a new religious club. But even here there is no distinction made between a false profession of Christ and a true profession of Christ. A true profession is assumed, but the contrast is between pagan unbelief and Christian belief.

Spurious Christianity as opposed to the real thing is not under discussion.

The third and last application of the name *Christian* comes from within the body of Christ, and it shows that the name has stuck. The apostle Peter, when writing to a body of believers, tells them that they should not suffer as evildoers. They have left that way of life behind. If any of them stumble into sin and suffer its consequences, then of course they should be ashamed of themselves.

> If ye be reproached for the name of Christ, happy are ye; for the spirit of glory and of God resteth upon you: on their part he is evil spoken of, but on your part he is glorified. But let none of you suffer as a murderer, or as a thief, or as an evildoer, or as a busybody in other men's matters. Yet if any man suffer as a Christian, let him not be ashamed; but let him glorify God on this behalf. For the time is come that judgment must begin at the house of God: and if it first begin at us, what shall the end be of them that obey not the gospel of God? (1 Pet. 4:14–17)

In the first part of this passage, Peter says that they are happy if they are "reproached for the name of Christ." He then says a moment later that if any man "suffer as a Christian," he should not be ashamed. It is difficult to miss the parallel. To be a Christian is to bear the name of Christ. If someone receives the world's hatred because he bears the name of a hated Christ, then there is no shame in it. Again, the judgment is being made from a distance—a persecutor hates Christ and attacks anyone associated with him.

These are the three places where the Bible indicates what the word *Christian* means. In two places, pagan unbelievers are applying the name to believers. In the third, an invitation is given to Christians to be in a certain frame of mind when persecutors come after them for being Christian. In all three places, the word is used by pagans. In Antioch, the pagans call the Christians by this name. In Paul's hearing, Agrippa speaks it in his summary of what he thinks Paul was trying to do to him. In the passage from Peter, an apostle imputes a hatred of the name of Christ, and this use of the word *Christian*, to pagan persecutors.

And this means we have no distinctively Christian handling of the word *Christian*. We have no direct teaching on what to make of statements like, "I grew up in the church but I became a Christian when I prayed a prayer something like this..." Here "becoming a Christian" means passing from one spiritual state to another, from darkness to light. It refers to conversion as an internal reality, but the Bible does not apply the word *Christian* to this or describe the process as that of becoming a Christian.

This of course does not mean that the subject is closed or that there is no such thing as genuine heart conversion. But it does mean that the remainder of the discussion, if it is to go beyond these three passages, is a matter of systematic and biblical theology and not a question of exegesis. Fortunately, we can still learn a great deal. But we have to be very careful as we undertake the task. The phrase "becoming a Christian" is strongly entrenched in our evangelical traditions and is an essential part of evangelical "systematics." Invariably, it is used to refer to the moment of regeneration.

Now such a moment is important to the teaching of Scripture as a whole, and, for each person, it is crucial to be able to answer the question of individual regeneration. The reason we have to address this is that in our culture many have grown up in the church: they were baptized in infancy or when they were ten in a Baptist church, they sang in the choir and went through catechism class, and they are not Buddhists. They have been Christians their whole lives. But if, like Nicodemus, they are not born again, what must they become? Does it make sense for them to "become a Christian?" There is *something* which they must become—spiritually alive. But how does the Bible describe this kind of change?

To answer the question, we have to look at some analogies from the Old Testament. There we see that someone could be outside the covenant entirely—a worshiper of Baal. A second category would be someone within the covenant people of Israel, who did not serve the God of Israel in truth. His service of God was externally formal and correct, but his heart was far from God. And lastly, there were true Israelites in whom there was no guile. Paul writes of this distinction at the end of the second chapter of Romans.

> For he is not a Jew, which is one outwardly; neither is that circumcision, which is outward in the flesh: But he is a Jew, which is one inwardly; and circumcision is that of the heart, in the spirit, and not in the letter; whose praise is not of men, but of God. (Rom. 2:28–29)

Circumcision was a sign of the covenant, but Paul points out that the mere possession of the external sign was not sufficient to guarantee a genuine spiritual reality. We can reapply these truths this way: "For he is not a Christian who is one outwardly; neither is that baptism, which is outward and external. But he is a Christian who is one inwardly; and baptism is that of the heart, in the spirit, and not in the letter; whose praise is not of men, but of God." Paul's statement is blunt—he is *not* a Christian who has only the externals. But we see in his next breath that Paul's statement was hyperbolic. Jews who had circumcision only were not Jews at all in one sense, but they were of course Jews in another. Lest anyone be tempted to think that this made external membership in the covenant a big nothing, Paul hastens to add that such membership was actually quite important.

> What advantage then hath the Jew? or what profit is there of circumcision? Much every way: chiefly, because that unto them

were committed the oracles of God. For what if some did not believe? shall their unbelief make the faith of God without effect? God forbid: yea, let God be true, but every man a liar; as it is written, That thou mightest be justified in thy sayings, and mightest overcome when thou art judged. (Rom. 3:1–4)

In other words, the religious world is filled with infidels at heart—people who were baptized in their childhood, but who do not believe any of the Christian faith now. Does this mean that their baptism—their "circumcision"—meant nothing? Not at all, Paul says. Every covenant member in the world could be lying about God through their lives, lives which contradict the religious signs which may have been applied to them at various points in their lives. Let God be true, Paul says, and every man a liar. That is all right—the truth remains firm.

The language can be pretty strong at times, as it ought to be. Those who carry Christian "marks" about with them, when they know nothing of the power of God in regeneration, are guilty of a very great sin. "I know thy works, and tribulation, and poverty, (but thou art rich) and I know the blasphemy of them which say they are Jews, and are not, but are the synagogue of Satan" (Rev. 2:9; cf. 3:9). In short, we can say that God knows those who call themselves Christians and who take upon themselves the marks of discipleship. Their lips are close to God, but their hearts are far from Him. Such are Christians covenantally, but their lives betray that covenant. This does not make God false—it would take more liars among men than we could come up with to accomplish that—but it does show that the word *Christian* can be used in two senses.

A Christian, in one sense, is anyone who has been baptized in the name of the Father, Son and Holy Spirit by an authorized representative of the Christian church. Does this mean that anyone so baptized is a Christian in the other sense—one who is born of the Spirit of God? Not at all. Again, we can take an illustration from the Jews. It is not "as though the Word of God hath taken none effect. For they are not all Israel, which are of Israel" (Rom. 9:6). To apply Paul's distinction here, they are not all the Christian church who are *of* the Christian church. There are those who are covenantally of the Church, but who are not individually regenerate. And if someone dies apart from that regeneration which brings us out of our native condition of spiritual death, such a person is lost eternally. In other words, Christians in the first sense alone are condemned to hell. As Jesus put it, "You *must* be born again."

External badges of Christian obligations do not get someone "halfway there." They are not "better than nothing." They are far, far worse than nothing. It would be better to have never formed any kind of attachment to Christ at all than to form a false one. And this is why Sodom got off easier than Capernaum (Mt. 11:24).

This means that if someone has been a Christian his whole life, but then comes into the new life that Christ presented to Nicodemus, we can say that he has become a Christian inwardly. He has now been baptized inwardly. He has become a Christian in truth. And if we know what we are saying, and we qualify it as Paul did, we might even say that he has become a Christian. However this would be comparable to a man who was married for ten years but was regularly unfaithful, who finally had a real change of heart. After ten years, he might say, as might his wife, that on the day he repented he finally became a husband. And he did—he finally knows what it is all about. But we need to remember that covenantally he was a husband all along, and had all the obligations of marriage.

And this means that many Christians need to become Christian all the way through. The applications move in two directions and forbid two grievous errors. Of course, these two errors (when committed) play off each other, which is why we must hold fast to the Scriptures. The first error is that of individualistic pietism, assuming that invisible saints are the only saints, or, rather, that invisible saintliness is the only kind. Advocates of the "ethereal Church" need to learn that, according to the Bible, a Christian is one who would be identified as such by a Muslim. Membership in the Christian faith is objective—it can be photographed and fingerprinted.

The opposing error is that of straight hypocrisy. This is the idea that mere covenant membership can replace covenant faithfulness as the one thing needful. The lips draw near while the heart is far removed from God. But such snakes within the covenant have the worst lot of all.

2

Calvinistic Bona Fides

When we talk about the covenant, we must always remember that God is the sovereign Lord of the covenant. Covenantal faithfulness on our part means remembering, constantly, the *Godness* of God. But before we go on to have some typical contemporary "Calvinist" assumptions challenged by the authority of this sovereign God, it is important to remember how effectively and completely God challenged our previous "non-Calvinist" assumptions. In other words, we want to grow our roots deeper into sovereign grace, which is a different thing from being blown about by every wind of doctrine.

The Bible teaches the exhaustive sovereignty of God. It does so in countless places, but one place where the summary is gloriously made is in the first chapter of Ephesians. "In whom also we have obtained an inheritance, being predestinated according to the purpose of him who worketh all things after the counsel of his will" (Eph. 1:11).

As we think about these things we have to make the connection between easy assumptions and hard consequences. Most Christians do not have a problem acknowledging God's control over the physical creation. Not a sparrow falls to the ground apart from the Father, and He foreordained the number of atoms that make up the planet Jupiter, along with their current locations. What Christians *do* have a problem with are the consequences of saying this, with particular regard for our own prideful choices. What does this doctrine look like when spread out into the corners? We do not begin understanding the objectivity of the covenant by inching away from black-coffee Calvinism; rather, we begin by asserting it in the strongest possible terms. God is the God of *everything*.

We do have free choices, but they are all under God. Modern Christians like to say that He has the whole world in His hands—which in our folly we make our personal comfort when we want and a grand theological discomfort the rest of the time. But there are countless passages which assert this; let us consider just a few. Job spoke the truth about a man's life when he said "seeing his days are determined, the number of his months are with thee, thou hast appointed his bounds that he cannot pass" (Job 14:5). Until that day arrives which God has established, every man is immortal.

As far as God's determination is concerned, we cannot lengthen or shorten our lives. Humanly speaking, can we? Of course. But whatever we do will not alter God's decree—whatever we do will be *His* instrument for accomplishing *His* decree, a decree that was settled before the worlds were made. We have the same teaching elsewhere (e.g. Ps. 139:16). Before we were born, our biography was already written. And this was not a sketch of the broad outlines either. "The preparations of the heart in man, and the answer of the tongue, is from the Lord" (Prov. 16:1).

What is more indicative of a man's freedom than that which he wills to speak? When you ask him a question, he answers the way he wishes. Is God somewhere else? No, God is Lord of all.

And yes, this even includes our sin. Many people have a problem with God's control of free actions because they do not want to say that men are nothing more than puppets. We think we should have a problem with God's control of sin because we think that this would make God Himself sinful.

But first, the teaching of Scripture: "But as for you, ye thought evil against me; but God meant it unto good, to bring to pass, as it is this day, to save much people alive" (Gen. 50:20; see also Is. 45:7 and Amos 3:6). Remember how Jesus foretold Peter's denial (Mk. 14:30). This does not exclude human responsibility for sin. "And truly the Son of Man goeth, as it was determined: but woe unto that man by whom He is betrayed!" (Lk. 22:22). God's sovereignty over sin involved far more than simply Judas. "For of a truth against thy holy child Jesus, whom thou hast anointed, both Herod, and Pontius Pilate, with the Gentiles, and the people of Israel, were gathered together, for to do whatsoever thy hand and thy counsel determined before to be done" (Acts 4:27–28).

Nothing happens outside the decretive will of God. But because one charge against those who hold to the objectivity of the covenant is that we are drifting away from predestinarian foundation of the Reformed faith, a few additional comments on the Westminster Confession are necessary at this point. The Westminster Confession of Faith speaks of God's sovereignty this way.

> God from all eternity, did, by the most wise and holy counsel of His own will, freely, and unchangeably ordain whatsoever comes to pass: yet so, as thereby neither is God the author of sin, nor is violence offered to the will of the creatures; nor is the liberty or contingency of second causes taken away, but rather established. (3:1)

This refers to what is usually called predestination, but should more properly be called foreordination. The word *predestination* is usually applied in Scripture to the surety that the elect will be brought by God to the resurrection of the body. But the truth represented by the common use of this word is sure; before the world was made, from all eternity, God decreed the number of hairs on that yellow dog's back, the one across the street. This is something He did in all wisdom. What was so decreed is therefore settled, both freely and unalterably.

This was done in such a way that God cannot be charged with sin. This is of course true by definition, but it is important to re-iterate the point. God is the Creator of a world which is now full of sin, and yet He cannot be charged with the guilt of it. The Confession says that God ordains that sinful action *x* will take place, and yet He is not the author of it. Another position holds that God foreknows *x*, and yet is not the author of it. Still an-other position says that God does not know the future and cre-ated the world anyway. But if men can charge God with being implicated in evil, then they may with justice continue to charge Him as long as the doctrine of creation is affirmed. There is no escape; if God is the Creator, then He is responsible for the pres-ence of *x*. We might as well face it.

At the same time, this does not make God the master pup-peteer. What He foreordained was a world full of free choices. He not only ordained that a man would be in the ice cream store choosing one of thirty-one flavors, He also decreed which flavor he would choose. But that is not all; He ordained that the cookie dough ice cream would be chosen by this man *freely*. God ordains *noncoercively*. This makes no sense to some people, but how many basic doctrines do make sense? We do not understand how God made the solar system from nothing any more than how He determined my actions today without annihilating me. But He did. Remember, the point being made here is not that divine sovereignty is merely consistent with secondary freedom but rather is that which *establishes* it.

> Although God knows whatsoever may or can come to pass upon all supposed conditions, yet hath He not decreed any thing because He foresaw it as future, or as that which would come to pass upon such conditions. (3:2)

God does foreknow all things, and He knows all the possibilities and contingencies. And yet we are not to suppose that God foreordains anything based upon His knowledge of what the world would have done without Him anyway. He does not peer down the corridors of time, see what is happening, and then decree that it will happen just as it would have happened anyway.

> By the decree of God, for the manifestation of His glory, some men and angels are predestinated unto everlasting life; and others foreordained to everlasting death. (3:3)

God does what He does, by His decree, and for His glory. This includes the apportionment of everlasting life, both to men and angels. Some are predestined to life, while others are foreordained to everlasting death. The use of different verbs here is significant. God's predestination to life is assigned to men who are in a state of death. God's decision to leave someone in his death is different in kind from His decision to remove someone from that death. Consider ten men on death row, all of whom deserve to die. The governor, for good and sufficient reasons, decides to pardon three of them. Has he done an injustice to the other seven? His action affects all ten, but his action toward the three is of a different nature than his lack of action toward the seven.

> These angels and men, thus predestinated, and foreordained, are particularly and unchangeably designed, and their number so certain and definite, that it cannot be either increased or diminished. (3:4)

This paragraph in the Confession keeps men from trifling with the words—which, on a subject like this, they always want to do. Because the word *predestination* is in the Bible something must be done with it, and men try to make the elect an elastic category. But we are basically dealing with two lists of names which are fixed. The lists do not grow or shrink, and names on the lists cannot be exchanged.

> Those of mankind that are predestinated unto life, God, before the foundation of the world was laid, according to His eternal and immutable purpose, and the secret counsel and good pleasure of His will, hath chosen, in Christ, unto everlasting glory, out of His mere free grace and love, without any foresight of faith, or good works, or perseverance in either of them, or any other thing in the creature, as conditions, or causes moving Him thereunto: and all to the praise of His glorious grace. (3:5)

This is a fine statement of unconditional election, which is entirely different from arbitrary or capricious election. The truth being insisted upon here is that God has no reasons that He found in *us* that are the basis of His election of us. He has many reasons, all of them good, for His selection. He does what He does according to His secret counsel and the good pleasure of His will. Further, the choice springs from His grace and love. This means that God has compelling reasons for election—it is not a question of *eeny, meeny, miney, moe*. But the good reasons do *not* include foresight of our faith, good works, stamina in either, good looks, or anything else that might be found in the creature which would enable him to boast.

> As God hath appointed the elect unto glory, so hath He, by the eternal and most free purpose of His will, foreordained all the means thereunto. Wherefore, they who are elected, being fallen in Adam, are redeemed by Christ, are effectually called unto faith in Christ by His Spirit working in due season, are justified, adopted, sanctified, and kept by His power, through faith, unto salvation. Neither are any other redeemed by Christ, effectually called, justified, adopted, sanctified, and saved, but the elect only. (3:6)

If God has elected these (and only these) to salvation, then why pray, preach, or witness? The answer is that God does not just predestine the end, which is, for example, the salvation of Smith. He also predestined, as a necessary part of the whole process, the varied preconditions and means which were necessary to bring Smith to the point of salvation. These preconditions included being fallen in Adam, redeemed by Christ, and called and kept by the Holy Spirit. The elect have all the preconditions preordained for them, and those who are not elect do not participate in the foreordained salvific preconditions.

> The rest of mankind God was pleased, according to the unsearchable counsel of His own will, whereby He extendeth or withholdeth mercy, as He pleaseth, for the glory of His sovereign power over His creatures, to pass by; and to ordain them to dishonour and wrath for their sin, to the praise of His glorious justice. (3:7)

If it is done according to the unsearchable counsel of His own will, then we should not try to search it out. We may assert it because the Bible does, but cannot plumb the depths of His counsel at this point. God may withhold mercy without injustice. If mercy could be demanded as a matter of justice, then it would no longer be mercy. Mercy and grace can never be demanded as a right. Why does God pass by some of His creatures, leaving them in their sin? He does so in order to manifest His justice, which is glorious. In order for justice to be manifested, it is necessary that sinners fall under dishonor and wrath. In a world without sin, two of God's most glorious attributes—His justice and His mercy—would go undisplayed. This, obviously, would be horrible.

> The doctrine of this high mystery of predestination is to be handled with special prudence and care, that men, attending the will of God revealed in His Word, and yielding obedience thereunto, may, from the certainty of their effectual vocation,

be assured of their eternal election. So shall this doctrine af-
ford matter of praise, reverence, and admiration of God; and of
humility, diligence, and abundant consolation to all that sin-
cerely obey the Gospel. (3:8)

This truth should be handled gingerly. Sinners like to blame
God instead of themselves, and they do so with particular impu-
dence whenever they are made aware of these truths about
God's sovereignty. But the reason we emphasize it is threefold.
First, we must understand this in order to make our calling and
election sure. Secondly, it gives rise to many occasions where
God may be greatly glorified. Lastly, this teaching is a humbler
of proud men. Those who are proud of their knowledge of this
doctrine (as opposed to all those modern evangelical "clothheads"
out there) have the worst of all situations. The most obvious thing
about predestination is that it exalts God and abases the creature. But this is not be confused with the exaltation of the creature who *pretends* to exalt God. As John Newton put it,

> And I am afraid there are Calvinists, who, while they account it
> a proof of their humility that they are willing in words to de-
> base the creature, and to give all the glory of salvation to the
> Lord, yet know not what manner of spirit they are of. Whatever
> it be that makes us trust in ourselves that we are comparatively
> wise or good, so as to treat those with contempt who do not
> subscribe to our doctrines, or follow our party, is a proof and
> fruit of a self-righteous spirit. Self-righteousness can feed upon
> doctrines, as well as upon works; and a man may have the heart
> of a Pharisee, while his head is stored with orthodox notions of
> the unworthiness of the creature and the riches of free grace.[†]

In no way is the objectivity of the covenant inconsistent with
these truths about God's sovereignty. In no way am I backing
away from high-octane Calvinism. There will be things written
later in this book which may *look* as though this is happening, but

[†] *The Works of John Newton* (Carlisle, Penn.: Banner of Truth, 1985 [1820]),

the reader should be assured that it is not. The point of this section has been to establish foundational Calvinistic bona fides. Doctrinal prejudice may still refuse to see how the harmonization works, *but the harmonization is still there*. So the reason for covering this ground again is that some have assumed (readily and wrongly) that the objectivity of the covenant poses a threat to the Reformed faith. In reality, it *is* the historic Reformed faith. The resolution of the RPCUS in the summer of 2002 stated that the doctrinal views I am arguing for here involve a redefinition of "the Church, the sacrament, election, effectual calling," along with many other doctrines central to the Reformed faith. The goal here is to establish that this is a gross misunderstanding.

And so how does divine sovereignty apply to the question of the covenant? Whatever we learn from Scripture about membership in the covenant, hypocritical attachment to the covenant, or perseverance in the covenant, *all of it* is from the hand of God, and is the outworking of the good counsel of His will. *Nothing* is an afterthought for Him. Not only is God true if every man is a liar, God is the sovereign over all those liars. In this book, we are considering how the sovereign God orders the covenant; we are *not* entertaining the view that God orders some things and leaves others to chance, free will, or some other will o' the wisp.

I referred earlier to one of the frequently quoted "mottos" of the Reformation—*ecclesia reformata et semper reformanda*—the Church reformed and always reforming. Hidebound tradition and spontaneous innovation do not go together, but there is another combination which does. We desire to see the Church reformed—zeal for novelty is a sinful desire. Our deep desire should be to walk in the old paths in the right way. But we also desire to see her always reforming—Jesus taught us that *faithfulness* is the basis for godly originality and not some spark of "creativity" (Mt. 13:52). When a tree grows, it is not innovating. But it is not dead either.

3

Evangelical Bona Fides

In learning the meaning of the covenant, we will of necessity have to unlearn a few things. But the temptation is ever present to "unlearn" too much, failing to live up to what we have attained. This tendency to "overshoot" is what makes some theological conservatives nervous about any changes at all.

There are three main areas where we must be careful— the sovereignty of God was affirmed in the last chapter, but two others remain. This chapter addresses the nature and necessity of the new birth, and the following chapter will address the centrality of *sola fide*. Put another way, growing in our covenant understanding does not entail abandoning historic Calvinism, nor does it mean jettisoning the historical evangelical faith or the historic Reformed faith.

Simply put, the objectivity of the covenant does *not* mean that a man does not have to be born again. And this means we must consider the nature of the new birth. "He that believeth on the Son hath everlasting life: and he that believeth not the Son shall not see life; but the wrath of God abideth on him" (Jn. 3:36).

The Scriptures teach that there are two kinds of people ultimately, not to mention four kinds of people in the meantime. At the end of history, the human race will have been divided into two categories, the inhabitants of heaven and hell respectively. Those who have everlasting life *then* are those who received everlasting life here, those who believed on the Son. Those on whom the wrath of God remains are those who did not believe the Son.

The picture is complicated, however, by two additional historical variables—what about those who *say* they believe (through baptism) but do not really believe? And what about those who believe but have not yet been baptized? The following table summarizes the four basic categories.

	Believers	**Unbelievers**
Covenant Members	*Covenant Keepers*	*Covenant Breakers*
Nonmembers	*Catechumens*	*Heathens*

What we are talking about emphasizes the importance of history and sanctification within history. Our constant temptation is to speak and think as though the categories of the *eschaton*—the sheep and goats of the last day—are visible and apparent to us here now at a glance. But this is far too facile. Such truths are *made* visible over time, in history, as the Spirit works in the Church. Such truths are not made *true* over time, but they are made *visible*. With our two separate categories, which is the lens for viewing the other?

The modern evangelical tendency is to assume that we have the ability to see the heart, and we then look at covenant membership through the lens of that mysterious ability. But we cannot see the heart. We cannot see regeneration, where it comes from, or where it goes. Our Lord taught us that we cannot see the wind blowing. We can have some idea of its effects, but this is not the same thing.

Jesus taught Nicodemus that a man must be born again (Jn. 3:3). Nicodemus was a covenant member, and a teacher in Israel. He should have known about this already, and the Lord chides him for missing it. The Lord then phrased it another way—a man must be born of water and of the Spirit (3:5). And Jesus does not just limit this to individual men—*all Israel* must be born again (3:7), which is what happened at Pentecost. The valley of dry bones was transformed, and Israel stood up again, filled with resurrection life. But of course a rebirth of all Israel also depends on the transformation of individual men and women. This corporate regeneration of the people of God in no way lessens the need for individuals to be born of the Spirit of God. How could a call for omelettes be taken as opposition to eggs?

When considering issues of life and death, the distinguishing feature here is belief. The one who believes does not perish, but has everlasting life (3:15–16). The one who refuses to believe is condemned already (3:18). Now the Bible teaches, from beginning to end, that genuine belief and *claims* to belief are not necessarily identical. Men often say one thing with their lips while their hearts are far from God (Mt. 15:7). *And they do the same thing with their participation in the sacraments.* So the division at the last day is saving faith on the one hand (Jn. 3:36), and spurious faith and overt unbelief on the other (Jas. 2:19; Jn. 3:19–20).

Everlasting life cannot be contained in a bottle. The wind blows where it wants (3:8). You can hear it, but *cannot* tell where it comes from or where it is going. *This is what the birth of the Spirit is like*—we must pray to God that He enables us to hear these words. Why must we choose between those who deny the new birth and those who affirm it glibly—do they not have it wrapped up in this little package, one that has three or four neat little steps? Modern evangelicals write books on *How to Be Born Again*, which betrays the fact that they are not grasping the Lord's teaching in the third chapter of John. Does anyone write books on how to be born the first time? Who would buy it?

But at the same time, liberals and mere formalists want to deny the living reality of new life that is brought to sinful men and women—both inside the covenant and outside it—by the power of God. We have to take care to resist both errors. First, *the new birth is a reality.* To be born again separates those who love darkness and those who love the light. But second, *the new birth is a mystery.* To be reborn of water and the Spirit is not something we have the ability to label and track.

On this subject, we tend to want the applications to have a tidy "how-to" check list attached. But that's too bad. One mistake might be called *mystery through ignorance*—Nicodemus was befuddled by all of this, but in the wrong way. He was a teacher in Israel and should not have been baffled in the way he was. Another error is *"knowledge" through ignorance*—pop evangelicalism has rushed in where Nicodemus feared to tread. We know *all* about it and will tell you how to get born again right now: one, two, three, drive a stake in the ground, what's the problem?

The right response here is *mystery through knowledge.* Historic evangelicalism has affirmed both the reality and mystery of God's new creation of faith in the world, in the hearts of sinful men, women and children. When addressing the effectual call of individual men and women, the Westminster Confession said this:

> All those whom God hath predestinated unto life, and those only, He is pleased, in His appointed and accepted time, effectually to call, by His Word and Spirit, out of that state of sin and death, in which they are by nature to grace and salvation, by Jesus Christ; enlightening their minds spiritually and savingly to understand the things of God, taking away their heart of stone, and giving unto them an heart of flesh; renewing their wills, and, by His almighty power, determining them to that which is good, and effectually drawing them to Jesus Christ: yet so, as they come most freely, being made willing by His grace. (10:1)

All those and only those. The triune God does not work at variance with Himself in the work of salvation. Those predestinated unto life are the same who are called. They are called because God is pleased to do so, and is pleased to do so when and how He has determined. In other words, it is not just the salvation of Smith which pleases Him, but also the manner and time in which Smith comes. One constant is the fact that God calls by His Word and by His Spirit. Those saved are called out of their natural state, which is one of sin and death, and they are called into grace and salvation. Of course, all is done through Jesus Christ.

The result of this call is that their minds are enlightened so that they might understand the things of God. God takes away their stony heart, and gives them a new heart. It is worth noting yet again that if a man could repent and believe with his old heart, he doesn't really need a new one. God renews and quickens his will, orients him to the good, and efficaciously draws him to Christ. But the fact that God draws him efficaciously does not mean that he is made into a robot or puppet. He comes most freely, genuinely wanting the salvation which God gave him the desire for.

This is not a true desire, some might say, if God gives it. Is desire for food true desire? Who gives that? Is desire for sexual relations true desire? Who gives that?

> This effectual call is of God's free and special grace alone, not from anything at all foreseen in man, who is altogether passive therein, until, being quickened and renewed by the Holy Spirit, he is thereby enabled to answer this call, and to embrace the grace offered and conveyed in it. (10:2)

No trickery or time travel may be used to get around the supremacy of God in this. God does not look down the corridors of time, see people choosing Him, and then choose them as a consequence. This effectual call is all of God, and man has no part in it—other than to benefit from the gift of it. Man is altogether passive until after the gift is given. Once the Holy Spirit quickens and renews him, he is then able to respond to the gift. Consequently, the *hierarchical* order is effectual call, regeneration, repentance, faith in the gospel, and salvation. (I am aware of the

theological problems inherent in trying to put a stopwatch
to this process of conversion. This order should simply be understood as systematic illustration designed to resist every
form of syncretism.)

> Elect infants, dying in infancy, are regenerated, and saved by
> Christ, through the Spirit, who worketh when, and where, and
> how He pleaseth: so also are all other elect persons who are in-
> capable of being outwardly called by the ministry of the Word.
> (10:3)

With a great deal of practical wisdom, the Confession says nothing about the state of infants who die as infants, other than to say
that some of the elect are found among them. Where the Bible is
silent, so should we be. Such infants (and others, like those severely retarded) are regenerated and saved by Christ, through
the Spirit, even though we cannot see the outward ministry of
the Word. In this, as with all things, God remains King and Sovereign.

> Others, not elected, although they may be called by the minis-
> try of the Word, and may have some common operations of the
> Spirit, yet they never truly come unto Christ, and therefore
> cannot be saved: much less can men, not professing the Chris-
> tian religion, be saved in any other way whatsoever, be they
> never so diligent to frame their lives according to the light of
> nature, and the laws of that religion they do profess. And to as-
> sert and maintain that they may, is very pernicious, and to be
> detested. (10:4)

The nonelect who hear the ministry of the Word cannot patch
together their own salvation from those things which they hear
and experience. They may even experience some common operations of the Spirit but not be saved at the last day. But note
that, according to the Westminster theologians, a man could be
called by the ministry of the Word and yet not be saved. He

could possess some common operations of the Spirit and yet ultimately be lost. This is the kind of man that has created our controversy: he is a covenant member, called by the Word, touched by the Holy Spirit, and yet he is lost. If this can happen, still less can someone patch together a code of conduct from the light of nature and whatever Tao they may happen to possess. Their diligence in patching this together will be revealed in the last day as no diligence at all. To surmise that men can be saved apart from the efficacious operation of the gospel is, our fathers tell us, a mischievous error, and a detestable one.

We see in this portion of the Confession that a man is "quickened and renewed" in such a way as to enable him to respond to the call of God. This might be called regeneration, theologically considered. A man is either regenerate or he is not. When the word *regeneration* is being used in this sense, we are talking about an invisible operation performed by the Spirit of God, who does what He does when and how it pleases Him. And when we are talking about what might be called this "effectual-call-regeneration," we have to repudiate every form of baptismal or decisional regeneration. We do not control the Spirit of God at the baptismal font any more than we control Him with our spiritual laws booklets.

At the same time, this is not the only legitimate use of the term *regeneration*.

John Calvin, however, uses the term regeneration in a much broader, more inclusive sense, comprehending not only the first inception of the new life in Christ, but also the manifestations of this new life throughout life. In other words, regeneration, or spiritual renewal, as used by Calvin, includes not only the origin of the new life, but also sanctification, the process of development or growth in the new life. "That this may be more clear," Calvin says, "let my readers call to mind that there is a twofold grace in baptism, for therein both remission of sins and regeneration are offered to us. We teach that full remission is made, but that regeneration is only begun, and goes on making progress during the whole of life."[1]

In this Calvinistic sense, baptism offers a twofold grace—forgiveness of sins and regeneration. In this *limited* sense, we can say that Calvin held to baptismal regeneration. But he also believed in the effectual call, and he knew (being a good Calvinist, perhaps even the best) that this effectual call could precede or follow the moment of baptism.

> If we wish to restrict the first of these two senses to the term regeneration, in accord with present-day Reformed thought, and to call the latter "sanctification," or if you please, Christian nurture, all well and good. But both of these senses are included in the significance of the baptism of infants, in Calvin's thought. In his mind there was no contradiction in assuming that children of the covenant were baptized in view of the fact that they were truly the children of God, truly regenerated, and yet, that they were also baptized into the continued process of regeneration, in future Christian experiences.[2]

In conclusion, what God does in His mysterious saving operations, God offers in His sacraments. When we see His promises there, it is not because we are being superstitious but rather the reverse. We are taking Him at His Word. Nicodemus was circumcised, but did not know about the new birth—both of Israel, and of individual Israelites. Many have been baptized and have not known the reality offered in that baptism. The problem is not that they have the baptism, but rather that they do not have the faith. For a man must be born again if he is to see the kingdom of heaven.

[1] Lewis Schenck, *The Presbyterian Doctrine of Children in the Covenant* (New Haven: Yale UP, 1940), 8–9. Schenck's citation of Calvin is from *Acta Synodi Tridentinae: Cum Antidoto per Joann. Calvinum* (1547.) *Corpus Reformatorum, Volumen XXXV*, 425.
[2] Ibid., 20–21.

4

Reformation Bona Fides

We have seen that the objectivity of the covenant does not require that we abandon our understanding of the majesty and sovereignty of God—just the opposite. Nor does it call for us to walk away from the glory and power of the Holy Spirit's regenerating work in the hearts of men, women and children. And, as we will consider here, it does not mean abandoning or backing away from the biblical and historic doctrine of *sola fide*. But we have to make all such qualifications because *current* misunderstandings of the covenant do need to be modified—and when we do, some will be tempted to think we are compromising on some of these basics.

Paul teaches us that salvation is by faith, from first to last. "For I am not ashamed of the gospel of Christ: for it is the power of God unto salvation to every one that believeth; to the Jew first, and also to the Greek. For therein is the righteousness of God revealed from faith to faith: as it is written, The just shall live by faith" (Rom. 1:16–17).

The gospel of Christ, as Paul indicates here, is nothing to be ashamed of. Why? It is the power of God unto salvation to every one who believes. This comes first to the Jew and then to the Greek. In this gospel, the righteousness of God is manifested—and this in at least two senses. The *nature* of the gospel reveals how it is that God can be righteous in the saving of sinners (Rom. 3:26). He can justify us without ceasing to be just. But it also reveals the righteousness of God *in how we who are saved by faith actually live*. Now given this, *how* can this righteousness be manifested? From faith to faith, and, we might add, on faith and under faith, through faith and by faith. "The just shall live by faith," not "the just shall start out by faith." The righteousness of God is also revealed in His faithfulness to the covenant—He promised this to Abraham.

Nothing is more commonplace than for us to say that we are saved by grace through faith (Eph. 2:8–9). This has achieved the status of an evangelical cliché. Like many clichés, and like all *scriptural* clichés, it is quite true. But also like many clichés, the actual truth expressed may be unknown to the person expressing it (Prov. 26:7). There are too many ways for us to bring in assumptions we are unaware of. We are saved by grace through faith, which is not the same thing as *faithlessly* clutching a proposition that we are saved by grace through faith. Too many professing Christians think that salvation by grace is actually salvation by tiny works.

The temptation—from the very beginning—has been to see faith as a point in time affair, after which the work of sanctification takes over. The Galatians stumbled into thinking this way: "Are ye so foolish? having begun in the Spirit, are ye now made perfect by the flesh?" (Gal. 3:3). Paul exhorts the Colossians in a similar way. "For though I be absent in the flesh, yet am I with you in the spirit, joying and beholding your order, and the steadfastness of your faith in Christ. As ye have therefore received Christ Jesus the Lord, *so* walk ye in him: rooted and built up in him, and stablished in the faith, as ye have been taught, abounding therein with thanksgiving" (Col. 2:5–7). As you have received—so walk. We must *continue* the way we began. We must *walk* the way we received. How? From faith to faith.

The Bible says that the just shall live by faith, but this entails the fact that the just shall *live*. What analogy shall we use? Faith as the starting gun of a race makes us fall into the Galatian error.

Faith as the foundation makes us think there are parts of the building that are supported ultimately by faith but are not themselves faith. All such illustrations set us up for a trap—law and gospel divisions or grace and works divisions. But we cannot divide the question of life and body the same way. Life permeates the whole man, and if it does not, then we do not have a man.

Faith is our *life*. But what is life? What is the difference between a dead man and a living man? They both have arms. They both have lungs. They may both have brown hair. Faith is life; unbelief is death, or the absence of such life.

And so it is never appropriate to "graduate" from faith. We are never to move on to other things. We are to live by faith. And what should we keep in mind as we do so? The Scriptures teach that *faith comes by hearing*—we cannot generate our own faith for the same reason we cannot generate our own life (Rom. 10:17). Take one of the great creeds for an example—some scholastic Protestants might want to know why the Apostles' Creed does not have "a section" on faith. They wonder if perhaps the confession was deficient in this respect. It is not, precisely because the early Christians were *confessing* their faith, not talking about it. The Creed begins with *credo*, "I believe." They are *doing* faith, not analyzing it. There was a place for analyzing faith, which our Protestant fathers had to do when resisting the destructive doctrines concerning merit in Roman Catholic theology. In the debate over soteriology, historic Protestant theology is right and merit theology of Roman Catholic theology is wrong. When confronting the same error, we have to respond in the same way. But we also have to remember that merit-mongering is not the only mongering possible. There is also the problem of *sola*-mongering. This error is committed when faith is honored and talked about endlessly—but not exercised.

Faith is responsive to the Word of God—Sarah provides us with the pattern (Heb. 11:11). Faith is the natural (and necessary) response to the perceived faithfulness of God. Unbelief is therefore to be thought of as a personal accusation against God.

The comment made above about "*sola*-mongering" does not mean that I am rejecting the *solas* of the Reformation—far from it. Rather, it is a recognition that every truth from God that ever appears in this sinful world always has two enemies. One is outside the camp and declares itself an enemy or adversary. The other is inside the camp and professes itself to be a friend. The controversy that swirls around the objectivity of the covenant exists in part because there are some who want *solas* they hold in their hand—which keeps those *solas* out of the heart and life and family. I do not deny the propositional truth the *solas* refer to, but I do maintain that to limit them to mere propositions is to kill them. Faith without works is dead. The five *solas* without works are dead too. Propositions without works are dead—even if the propositions are true.

Some might call this an innovation and say that it is inconsistent with the historic Reformed faith. Not exactly, and this brings us back to the Westminster Confession. Not only does this teaching not contradict the teaching of Westminster, it *is* the teaching of Westminster. There is a great irony to be found in the fact that the theology of modern Reformed Christians is often shaped more by Enlightenment categories than by the historic meaning of their own historic creeds. If a time traveler from the time of the Reformation showed up—say, one of the men who wrote the Westminster Confession—he would rapidly find himself brought up on charges for teaching things contrary to the Confession he helped to write.

> Those whom God effectually calls, He also freely justifieth; not by infusing righteousness into them, but by pardoning their sins, and by accounting and accepting their persons as righteous; not for any thing wrought in them, or done by them, but for Christ's sake alone; nor by imputing faith itself, the act of believing, or any other evangelical obedience to

> them, as their righteousness; but by imputing the obedience
> and satisfaction of Christ unto them, they receiving and resting
> on Him and His righteousness by faith; which faith they have
> not of themselves, it is the gift of God. (11:1)

In other words, God justifies those He calls, but this justification must *not* be understood as an infusion of righteousness.
Rather, justification is the pardon for sins and the legal reck-
oning of our persons as righteous. It is important that we do
not stumble through a misunderstanding of the basis or foundation of this. We are justified for Christ's sake only. God does
not justify us for anything done by us, and, far more important, for anything done in us (even by Him). Nor does God
justify us because of our faith—rather He justifies us because
of Christ's obedience and work, and this is appropriated by us
through faith. Understanding these prepositions (in the gut) is
a matter of life and death, heaven and hell.

This is what justification means. But it is important to note
that it is not the *only* thing it means. Theologically, however,
when we are talking about the justification of an elect *individual*,
this is what it means. Put another way, in the debate between
Protestants and Roman Catholics over the justification of an individual, the Protestants were right. But there are other questions. Was Jesus justified? Is the Church corporately justified?
Those questions will be addressed in a later chapter, but for now
it should be noted that nothing said there takes away from what
we believe here.

> Faith, thus receiving and resting on Christ and His righteous-
> ness, is the alone instrument of justification: yet is it not alone
> in the person justified, but is ever accompanied with all other
> saving graces, and is no dead faith, but worketh by love. (11:2)

We are saved through faith alone, but never through a faith that
is alone. Saving faith is never lonely. We can separate faith from

other graces and virtues logically and conceptually, via abstraction, but not practically. We may distinguish, but never separate.

Inability to make such distinctions without separating is what causes many to stumble over the relation of faith and works, or to use biblical terminology, faith and love. The kind of faith that God gives as a gift is always alive. And as a living reality, it does not die when the moment of justification is passed. That same faith, a gift from the same God, continues to work in the justified individual in his sanctification. Justification and sanctification are not the same thing, but they are appropriated by the same thing—living faith.

This is why faith alone is never alone. Faith is the only instrument God uses in our justification. But when God has done this wonderful work, the faithful instrument does not shrivel up and die. It continues to love God and obey Him. If it does not, but just lies there like a corpse, then we have good reason to believe that it was lying there like a corpse some days before—not being therefore an instrument of justification. Faith without works is a dead faith, and a dead faith never justified anybody. Saving faith is ever accompanied by all other *saving* graces.

> Christ, by His obedience and death, did fully discharge the debt of all those that are thus justified, and did make a proper, real, and full satisfaction to His Father's justice in their behalf. Yet, in as much as He was given by the Father for them; and His obedience and satisfaction accepted in their stead; and both, freely, not for any thing in them; their justification is only of free grace; that both the exact justice, and rich grace of God might be glorified in the justification of sinners. (11:3)

Pardon for sins is a great part of our justification. The debt for our sins was paid through Christ's obedience and death. On our behalf Christ genuinely satisfied the justice of the Father. Our justification reveals two aspects of God's nature and character—His justice displayed in Christ and His mercy displayed in Christ. In this great transaction, our sins were imputed to Christ and His righteousness imputed to us. The former reveals God's justice, the latter His mercy.

> God did, from all eternity, decree to justify all the elect, and Christ did, in the fullness of time, die for their sins, and rise again for their justification: nevertheless, they are not justified, until the Holy Spirit doth, in due time, actually apply Christ unto them. (11:4)

The decision to justify and the laying of the foundation for justifying are not the same as justifying. Again, we are talking here about *individual* justification which occurs at the moment an unconverted man is converted from darkness to light. We are not yet talking about corporate justification, which will be addressed later and does not contradict the realities of individual justification. Rather, it places those individual realities in a justified context.

> God doth continue to forgive the sins of those that are justified; and, although they can never fall from the state of justification, yet they may, by their sins, fall under God's fatherly displeasure, and not have the light of His countenance restored unto them, until they humble themselves, confess their sins, beg pardon, and renew their faith and repentance. (11:5)

Justification is permanent, and God never ceases to see a justified person as perfect. This has reference to the person's legal status; they are secure in their position within the family of God. And yet, because they are in the family of God, God does exhibit a fatherly displeasure for sin. It is the difference between having justification and having the *joy* of justification. A child awaiting a spanking in the basement is just as much a member of the family as he ever was. In fact, his secure membership in the family is the reason why he is in the basement (Heb. 12:8). However, it can be said that he is not happy about being a member of the family. When David falls under God's displeasure, he does not ask for his salvation back—he asks for the *joy* of his salvation back (Ps. 51:8,12).

> The justification of believers under the old testament was, in all these respects, one and the same with the justification of believers under the new testament. (11:6)

We cannot make a distinction between the saints of the Old Testament and the saints of the New in this respect. They may and do differ with regard to gifts and graces, but individual justification is the *sine qua non* of being a genuine saint of God.

In all this we are discussing, and reaffirming, the traditional Protestant doctrine of the righteousness of Christ imputed to those individuals who are elect. This, plus nothing, constitutes the ground of their final acceptance before God.

5

Tradition and Systematics

I think it was Charles Hodge who said that if something is true, it is not new, and if it is new, it is not true. In theology, innovation as such is no virtue. Our responsibility is to be faithful to the faith once for all delivered to the saints. At the same time, refusal to innovate must not be confounded with a refusal to *grow*. A student progressing from second grade to twelfth grade is learning "new" things, but the content of his lessons are not an innovation. In the same way over centuries the Church grows into deeper and richer understanding of the faith. In doing this, to be able to resist the charge of "innovation," the faithful have to be able to show the scriptural basis for the doctrinal practice as well as its general consistency with what has been learned before.

The Scriptures do not give us just one simple view of tradition.

> Now we command you, brethren, in the name of our Lord Jesus Christ, that ye withdraw yourselves from every brother that walketh disorderly, and not after the tradition which he received of us. (2 Thes. 3:6)

> Forasmuch as ye know that ye were not redeemed with corruptible things, as silver and gold, from your vain conversation received by tradition from your fathers. (1 Pet. 1:18)

Paul refers to the apostolic tradition of walking in an orderly manner, and Peter refers to the vain tradition of living in an empty and hollow way. The teaching of Scripture on tradition depends entirely on what that tradition is doing. As with other categories, we find that the words *good* and *evil* can both be applied. A husband can either be a good husband or a bad husband, depending upon what he is doing. A prophecy can either be true or false. We do not know until we hold it up to the standard God has given us, which is of course the Scriptures.

In the Thessalonians passage, Paul reminds the Thessalonians of the godly tradition which they had received from him. Peter tells his readers that the blood of Christ redeemed them from the empty way of life which they had inherited from their fathers by means of tradition. We see the same kind of thing when Christ rebuked the first-century Jews for their blind reliance on blind tradition (Mt. 15:1–9; Mk. 7:1–13; Col. 2:8). When this happens, the result is that the Word of God is supplanted.

A tradition is an *inheritance*. What you receive depends entirely on what was possessed by the one bequeathing that inheritance, as well as upon your understanding and appreciation of it. You might inherit a priceless china cabinet, or you might inherit an old greasy rag.

In the Christian era, three basic theologies of tradition have developed, and have been handed down—by tradition—to the present. In other words, we have three different traditions of tradition. These theologies, respectively, are (1) authoritative tradition as *equal* to Scripture, (2) authoritative tradition as *subordinate* to Scripture, and (3) tradition as *absolute*.[1] The first developed during the middle ages, and until recently was the consensus held in the Roman Catholic church. The second is the position of historic Protestantism. The third is the position held by individualist sectarians and by an increasing number in the modern Roman Catholic church.

[1] Keith Mathison, *The Shape of Sola Scriptura* (Moscow, Idaho: Canon Press,

The first says that Scripture and tradition are two streams of inspired truth. The second says that the traditions of the Church are authoritative, but are not infallible or ultimate. Only Scripture (*sola Scriptura*) has that position. The third position says that my (or our) interpretation of Scripture must by definition be correct. Historical continuity with *somebody* is simply assumed. Alexander Campbell, a leader in the restorationist movement of the nineteenth century, said that he endeavored to read every passage of the Bible as though he had never seen it before. Of course this just means that he had a very *short* tradition.

God created us in such a way that we do not have the luxury of a "no tradition" option. If we attempt it, the only thing we succeed in doing is incorporating a good deal of confusion into the tradition we hand down. This was seen by one wise Baptist pastor, who said, "We Baptists don't believe in tradition. It is contrary to our historic position." Our children grow up in our homes, and they learn countless lessons there—about worship, liturgy, devotion, cultural incarnation, and more. Most of what they know about these things is invisible to them. It is the teaching office of the Church, in part, to point out, identify, explain, and teach the biblical basis for such traditions. If there is no biblical basis for something, and the tradition is pernicious, then the point of the scriptural teaching should be in order to remove that tradition.

But the real pest is *nebulous* tradition. Traditions are at their worst when they grow up and are simply assumed in the bones, with no examination. But sinful human beings always need accountability—and sinful human opinions and traditions are the same. Those who compare themselves with themselves are not wise (2 Cor. 10:12). For example, a whole host of individualist traditions have grown up in the American church. We read our historic confessions through the eyes of this *recent* tradition. Many contemporary theologians and preachers read the Westminster Confession, for example, the way Supreme Court

justices read the Constitution. Their eisegesis is based on very
nebulous and unexamined oral traditions. In this way, the honest tradition of Westminster is supplanted by people with
modern inviso-traditions, who want the name of Westminster but not its doctrines.

> Those who pride themselves on being the orthodox are really
> the unorthodox. The Presbyterian Church has a glorious doc-
> trine received through the medium of John Calvin and the
> Westminster Standards. *Yet the Church as a whole does not know it.*
> The historic doctrine of the Church concerning children in
> the covenant and the significance of infant baptism has been to
> a large extent secretly undermined, hidden by the intrusion of
> an aberration from this doctrine.[2]

It is always our fashion to build memorials to the prophets
(Mt. 23:29–31), which shows our secret gladness in the fact
that they are all dead. Stephen was accused of being hostile to
Moses—though Luke makes it plain through a record of his
miracles and his radiant face that Stephen was the true heir of
Moses (Acts 6:8,15). In other words, Stephen was killed in the
name of Moses because he was far too much like Moses. The
more things change, the more they stay the same—in how many
modern Calvinist churches would John Calvin be brought up on
charges?

With regard to the doctrines of historic Protestantism, this
process has happened with the doctrine of Scripture, salvation
by faith alone, baptism, the Lord's Supper, and far more. We
have gotten to the point where if a man quotes John Calvin or
John Knox, modern Protestants think the citation must be from
the Council of Trent. In the modern, conservative wing of the
Protestant church, the chief culprit has been Enlightenment rationalism. Discussing the Lord's Supper, John Nevin describes

---

[2] Lewis Schenck, *Children in the Covenant*, 158. Emphasis mine.

one example of this out of many that could be cited.

> The very orthodoxy of the school now noticed was itself ra-
> tionalistic; and we may say of it, in this view, that it served only
> to precipitate the catastrophe which it sought to avert. For its
> conception of the supernatural was always external and ab-
> stract; placing it thus in the same false relation precisely to na-
> ture and humanity, which was established by Rationalism itself.
> This was to justify the wrong issue on which the controversy
> had been made to hang, and to make common cause in a cer-
> tain sense with the enemy, by consenting to meet him on his
> own ground, the arena of the mere finite understanding. No
> wonder, that the supernatural thus defended, was found un-
> able to sustain itself against the reigning tendency of the age.[3]

Now writing our traditions down in confessions and creeds
does not prevent a sinful reliance on them, but it does make the
process far more difficult. This is the case with confessions,
creeds, and authoritative systematic theologies. But inchoate
traditions, glib assumptions, and unexamined presuppositions
are extremely hard to identify. So there is an important place for
defined and formal interpretations, as long as we understand
what that place is. Along with the others—creeds and confessions—systematic theology has an important place. But it is not
the ultimate or only place, and it is false to say that no temptations come along with the study of systematics.

> It seems to me that to the degree that a particular systematic
> theology cannot speak the Gospel to the faithful as Scripture
> teaches us to speak that Gospel (e.g., 'baptism saves,' 'Jesus died
> for *you*,' 'take heed lest you fall,' etc.), to that degree the sys-
> tematic theology is deficient.[4]

---

[3] John Williamson Nevin, *The Mystical Presence* (Eugene: Wipf and Stock,
2000 [1846]), 138–139.

[4] S. Joel Garver, "Scriptural Indications" in *Taking Apostasy Seriously* [online collection of essays, hereafter *TAS*] <http://www.lasalle.edu/~garver/apostasy.htm>.

What this means is that systematic interpretations may be allowed to *interpret* what the Scriptures say (and indeed, we must do this), but they must never be allowed to *replace* what the Scriptures say. We can tell we have stumbled at this place when we disallow (for the sake of our systematic understanding) a phrase or statement that the Bible itself uses. In the citation above, Garver uses an example that tweaks the modern evangelical systematic understanding of baptism. The Bible says that baptism saves. Why do we not use this language? It is because our systematic language has replaced scriptural language. And although I hold to *sola fide* as the right scriptural interpretation, I have to do so recognizing that the only time the Bible uses the phrase "faith alone," it does so in order to deny it. "Ye see then how that by works a man is justified, and not by faith only" (Jas. 2:24).

> A wooden hermeneutic, which artificially restricts the way in which a word or concept may be employed, often results in a failure to appreciate the richness of that word or concept as it is used in the Bible. Ironically, the stiff approach is often employed as if it were a tool of orthodoxy when, in fact, it becomes a means by which the Word of God is abused.[5]

The question is not whether it is lawful to use systematic formulations to make our meaning clear. Of course it is lawful—from *homoousia* to *sola fide*, the orthodox are called to this. Heretics often wrap themselves in biblical terminology, and the orthodox frequently have to use phrases that are not found in the Bible anywhere, like *Trinity*. But in doing this, the orthodox are also called to remember that the Church has interpretive, ministerial authority, and not legislative authority. Attempts to *replace* scriptural terms are always outside the pale.

[5] Randy Booth, "Covenantal Antithesis" in *The Standard Bearer: A Festschrift for Greg Bahnsen,* ed. by Steve Schlissel (Nagadoches: Covenant Media Press, 2002), 62.

Such lawful interpretations can require technical and high-flown language. This is not necessarily bad, so long as we remember what we are doing.

> Reformed dogmatics from at least the seventeenth century onward was increasingly preoccupied with a rationalistic decretal theology that proceeded almost entirely from the perspective of God's eternal purposes. . . .Given the polemical context (the controversies with the Remonstrants and the Amaryldians), the preoccupation is understandable and was, for a time, helpful. It is not to be rejected out of hand.[6]

So what applications should we make? How can we be faithful to the Scriptures and to the *godly* traditions of our fathers? First, we begin and end with the gospel of sovereign grace. When the gospel confronts us, it leaves no wiggle room for sinners. God presents His salvation to us, in word and deed. We are commanded to fix our eyes on Jesus, the author and finisher of our faith. We will only do this faithfully if we see Him everywhere, but particularly in the *means of grace* that He has established so that we might commune with Him. When Christ calls, we must not try to answer the summons by hunting for a back door that will take us to Him. That back door will always be some form of self-righteous entry.

Second, assume that God has reserved for Himself far more faithful men and women down through history than you think. One of our modern traditions is a modification of the Elijah complex: "I am the only one left." But the Holy Spirit has been working constantly in the history of the Church since Pentecost, and the fact that His work looks "messy" to us is actually an indictment of *us*. God is perfect, but a glance at the universe shows that He is no perfectionist.

---

[6] S. Joel Garver, "Reformed Dogmatics" in *TAS*.

6

Individualism

Those who teach on the objectivity of the covenant tend to emphasize the dangers of individualism. As we continue to develop our understanding of the nature of the covenant, it is important for us to comprehend what we do not mean by this. We do not mean that individual believers are a nullity or that everything important must happen at the corporate covenant level. Again, the fact that we believe in a corporate covenant omelette does not mean we disbelieve in eggs.

> Then said Jesus unto his disciples, If any man will come after me, let him deny himself, and take up his cross, and follow me. For whosoever will save his life shall lose it: and whosoever will lose his life for my sake shall find it. For what is a man profited, if he shall gain the whole world, and lose his own soul? or what shall a man give in exchange for his soul? (Mt. 16:24–26)

There is no tension between omelettes and eggs. Christ is establishing His kingdom, and this kingdom has a corporate, covenant reality. But individuals are still called into this kingdom, one by one. Jesus says if "any man" wants to come after him, he must deny "himself," take up "his cross," and follow Christ. A man can save his own life, and thereby lose it. A man who loses his own life for the sake of Christ will then miraculously receive it back. A man gets no profit if he gains the world but loses his "own soul." If you lose your soul, then there is no "you" to own the world you gained. If you give your soul in exchange for anything, then when the accounts receivable come in, they arrive at a void.

As much as we reject individualism, we must take care not to overreact. After all, it is the individual who is the final "counting unit" whenever we consider judgment and justification. In other words, we go to heaven or hell by ones. "How is it with your soul?" is a reasonable and godly question, and one that pastors should ask more often than they do.

If a man denies himself to follow Christ, as commanded, if he denies himself in order to come into the community of the covenant, he therefore finds himself. Denying self is therefore the foundation of establishing the blessed life for godly individuals.

What is individualism then? In short, individualism is the deification of self. The "self" is looked to as the ultimate source of law, as the object of worship (service), and as the savior of self—the self becomes the center of an egocentric universe. But "there is a way which seemeth right unto a man, but the end thereof are the ways of death" (Prov. 14:12). Refusing to deny self is therefore a perverse annihilation of self. Individualism is therefore the mortal enemy of individuals.

We are what we are as individuals because of covenant relations. Within the covenant, we are what we are in relationship. The *koinonia* is the joint fellowship of the saints; our participation in Christ is experienced as relation with the head of the body and with the rest of the body necessarily. We are members of one another and are called to a life in which others are as dear as our own souls (1 Sam. 18:1–3; 20:17). This is the point of the commandment to husbands requiring them to love their wives as their own bodies (Eph. 5:28). And of course, we recall the second greatest commandment—"love your neighbor as yourself."

Our identity is bound up therefore with our covenant relationships and whose image we bear. A man is not defined by his internal essence. A man is not defined as an abstraction.

Everyone is someone's daughter or someone's son. We are married to someone and have sons and daughters. We are members of Christ and of one another. We are called to look in the mirror by looking around to see Christ—first in the gospel and secondly in our neighbor. And those who *see* Christ in both places *have* Christ.

So what are the different ways in which individualism makes war against our souls? Peter tells us to abstain from fleshly lusts, which war against the soul (1 Pet. 2:11). What kind of man loves his own soul? What kind of man despises his own soul? What kind of man loves himself—in the scriptural sense?

He is a humble man. The man who gets wisdom loves his *own soul* (Prov. 19:8). The man who keeps the commands of God keeps his *own soul* (Prov. 19:16). The salvation of the individual begins when the individual humbles himself (dethrones himself) and hears the words of wisdom.

Conversely, the man afflicted with stiff-necked pride is involved in self-destruction. The one sinning against wisdom wrongs his *own soul* (Prov. 8:36). The one who refuses instruction despises his *own soul* (Prov. 15:32). The one who refuses to acknowledge his own utter dependence on another to keep his own soul alive is a fool (Ps. 22:29).

Of course, there are also particular sins which reflect the deeper problems with pride and obstinacy. Resistance to teaching and wisdom leads to particular destructive sins. The adulterer hates his own soul (Prov. 6:32). The cruel man troubles his own flesh, while the merciful do good to their own souls (Prov. 11:17). The political agitator hates his own soul (Prov. 20:2). The one who is a companion of thieves hates his own soul (Prov. 29:24).

In summary, a man who loves his own soul will not bow down to it. A man who loves his individual soul will pursue wisdom, which cannot be pursued outside the corporate covenant boundaries of the Church.

Part II
Covenant, Church, and Sacraments

7

Defining the Covenant

We are arguing for the objectivity of the covenant. But how are we to define this objective covenant? We are seeking out how to "think covenantally." But we must be careful lest this turn into nothing other than "mindlessly reciting covenantally." The use of buzzwords advances nothing, and so we have to take care to ground what we are saying in the teaching of Scripture. Nowhere is this more important than in defining the word *covenant*. Our Bibles can be divided into two sections—the Old *Covenant* and the New *Covenant*, and yet many Christians would be hard put to define what this word is supposed to mean. What does *covenant* mean?

> Now the Lord is that Spirit: and where the Spirit of the Lord is, there is liberty. But we all, with open face beholding as in a glass the glory of the Lord, are changed into the same image from glory to glory, even as by the Spirit of the Lord. (2 Cor. 3:17–18)

We will begin with a working definition of *covenant*, and as we come to the various passages of Scripture, how the definition applies to the text quoted above will become clear. *Covenants among men are solemn bonds, sovereignly administered, with attendant blessings and curses.*

Christians tend to understand covenantal history one of two ways. Either God has made one basic covenant with men throughout history, or He has made more than one—possibly many. As we shall see, Scripture teaches that there is only one covenantal history, which we may call the *covenant of grace*. In the New Testament, we see the (final) scriptural name for this covenant is the *New Covenant*. But it is important to note at the outset of our discussion that this covenant of grace does not float above human history in some kind of ethereal way. The history of the covenant is intertwined with the rest of human history, including kings, battles, dates, and of course promises and sacraments.

Before the Fall, God had made a covenant with mankind in Adam, which we violated through our sin. Genesis of course tells us that Adam sinned against God, but Hosea tells us that Adam sinned against God *covenantally*. "But like men [*Adam*] they transgressed the covenant; there they dealt treacherously with Me" (Hos. 6:7). Hosea is complaining against the Israelites who were covenantally faithless, and in this, they were like Adam who had also been covenantally faithless. This faithlessness involved a real tree in a real garden, which then resulted in the expulsion of two real people. The Fall happened in history; the covenant with God was broken in history.

The subsequent redemptive covenant was equally grounded in history. Covenants are made by God with men in history. There is an aspect to such covenants which we may postulate as settled in the mind of God. For example, God knew and foreordained from before the foundation of the world who the elect would be at the end of the world. But this foreknowledge is not the covenant itself, but rather God's ultimate knowledge of the outcome of the covenant. But since we know that God has this knowledge, we have assumed that this is the "true" covenant made between God in His secret counsels and the elect, whoever *they* are. But this is not how the covenants are represented in the Bible. The covenants are historical and visible. Covenants of God have a physical aspect, like an oak tree.

After the Fall, God made covenants throughout the Old Testament. But they are not a series of disconnected covenants, as though God kept changing His mind about how to deal with men. His covenants unfold successively, and they cannot be understood apart from one another. Ultimately, they constitute the same covenant. The first was with *Adam and Eve* (Gen. 3:15). This was a messianic promise (e.g., Rom. 16:20), which means it must be understood covenantally. Then was the covenant with *Noah* (Gen. 6:18). Peter clearly tells us that this was a type and that Christian baptism is the antitype (1 Pet. 3:18–22).

We then come to *Abraham* (Gen. 17:2). As the New Testament tells us in multiple places, Abraham is the father of all who believe (Rom. 4:11). Moreover, the Bible tells us that if we are Christ's, then we are Abraham's seed and heirs according to the promise (Gal. 3:29). *Moses* is next and does not represent a covenantal detour (Exod. 2:24–25). Then we see *David* (2 Sam. 7:12–16). Who is the Christ? He is the Son of *David*.

All of these covenants find their ultimate fulfillment in the Lord of the covenant, that is, in Jesus Christ. The Old Covenant is not the time in which God attempted to save His people through law, but, finding this to be a failure, decided to use grace and forgiveness in the New Covenant. This understanding represents a radical misreading of the relationship of the two testaments.

A central part of our problem is caused by the New Testament refutations of the Pharisaical *distortions of* the law of Moses. They are commonly assaulted with their own (heretical) terminological distortions (i.e., words like "law"). But the contrast in the New Testament is not between Old and New; the contrast is between Old *distorted* and Old *fulfilled*. Tragically, many modern Christians agree with the Pharisees that their understanding of "the law" accurately represents the Old Testament. This is not the case at all—their view was a radical misreading of the Old Testament. Jesus did not praise them for reading the Old Testament correctly, but then urge them to adapt themselves to the coming changes. Rather, He rebukes them for *never* having had a clue.

Another difficulty is caused when well-meaning members of the "fulfillment party" see the arrival of the New Covenant as simply the next mundane step in covenant history. And it *is* the next step,but only in the same way the resurrection was "the next thing" after the crucifixion (Eph. 2:14–16). No one illustration captures it all—except for the reality of the cross and empty tomb.

The believer must think of the covenant as a growing child, a fruitful tree, a bud unfolding into a flower, but above all he must think of death and resurrection. We must understand the continuity of the covenants *only in this way.* That continuity is found in a Person, crucified and raised, and reflects the solitary redemptive purpose of God from the beginning of history to the end of it, always expressed in covenant. The Lord Jesus Christ is the Lord of the New Covenant now (Heb. 8:6); He has always been the Lord of the New Covenant (1 Cor. 10:1–13), and He ministers throughout all history (Heb. 9:15).

And so how are we to live? One of the great things we must note about God's covenantal faithfulness is that He has not done all these things in a corner. The sun has risen; why do we close our eyes in our introspection and complain that it is still dark? Looking *away* to God's mighty acts in history with faith *is not superstition.*

And here is the basis of *visible covenant faithfulness*—here is our central duty. Morbid introspection is a counterproductive fight with a tarbaby. Are you are Christian? Look by faith to Christ—in the Scriptures, in the preached Word, and in the sacraments.

This is what the text cited earlier pointed us to. We are to look to the glorious ministrations of the new covenant. As we do so, we are changed by the Holy Spirit from glory to glory.

Who also hath made us able ministers of the new testament; not of the letter, but of the spirit: for the letter killeth, but the spirit giveth life. But if the ministration of death, written and engraven in stones, was glorious, so that the children of Israel could not stedfastly behold the face of Moses for the glory of his countenance; which glory was to be done away: How shall not the ministration of the spirit be rather glorious? For if the ministration of condemnation be glory, much more doth the ministration of righteousness exceed in glory. (2 Cor. 3:6–9)

The glory of the new covenant is not an imaginary glory. Through the covenantal means established by God in the New Covenant, we are being transformed into the likeness of Jesus Christ, which process will culminate at the climax of the covenant, when God shall be all in all.

8

The Visible and Invisible Church

Whether we recognize it or not, we all have a pattern in our minds which we use to sort out the various competing religious claims we hear. Most of us as contemporary evangelicals frequently use the pattern of "visible and invisible" when thinking of the Church. Because of how we have used it, this has caused no small difficulty.

Before beginning this discussion it is important to acknowledge that the Church has aspects that are invisible to us.

> But ye are come unto mount Sion, and unto the city of the living God, the heavenly Jerusalem, and to an innumerable company of angels, to the general assembly and Church of the firstborn, which are written in heaven, and to God the Judge of all, and to the spirits of just men made perfect. (Heb. 12:22–23)

When we gather to worship on the Lord's Day, we do not *see* the "innumerable company of angels." Neither do we see all the people whose names are written in heaven or the spirits of just men made perfect. The Church is greater and more mysterious than can be taken in at a single glance. So of course, there are parts of the Church that we cannot see. Even in a local assembly there are aspects of the congregation which are invisible as well—emotions, thoughts, and the underside of the pews. It is no problem at all to acknowledge that the one Church has a visible and invisible aspect.

But there is a way to talk about this that can and does cause trouble. Since the time of the Reformation, Protestant Christians have been accustomed to speak of the visible Church and the invisible Church. The Westminster Confession, for example, speaks of the "catholic or universal Church, which is invisible" and defines this Church as consisting of the entire number of the elect (25:1). The visible Church is defined as all those who throughout the world "profess the true religion, together with their children" (25:2). This can be very helpful, but it can create a few problems. We cannot encourage others to be faithful to the covenant if we are ignoring the covenant.

In order to understand this, we have to refer to Hellenism again. The Hellenistic mind tends to see the ethereal, spiritual realm as the "real" one. That which is material and earthy is beneath all true philosophic consideration. There is a religious version of this about, and this is the attitude which sees the "invisible" Church as the "true" Church and the "visible" Church, at best, as only an approximation of the true Church. Down here on earth we might play at Church, but the real thing is invisible. When you have two churches existing at the same time, with the membership lists not identical, this creates a problem. We know there is only one Church, so which one is the real one? Modern evangelical Protestants have tended to say that the invisible Church is the real one, which is why we tend to have such a low view of the churches we can actually see.

It is not rare for individuals to refuse to have anything to do with the institutional Church, and, if called to account, defend themselves by saying that they are members of the invisible Church. This defense only works if the two churches are not the same and individuals here and now have the ability to see this invisible Church.

We are dealing with some unfortunate terms, and so we have to take care to define them. The heavenly Church is not invisible up *there*.[1] The worship services we attended in various sanctuaries last Lord's Day are *now* invisible to us. When we try to cobble the ethereal and material realms together, we find that we cannot do it because these are not scriptural categories. Not only is this so, but we also find ourselves now incapable of tying together the Church of today with the Church of yesterday, or tomorrow. The Church of yesterday is just as invisible as the heavenly Church. We lose the communion of the saints if we depend upon what we can see.

God knows who the elect are. If we simply say that the invisible Church is identical to the company of the elect, then this by itself does not create any problems. This is how the Westminster Confession defines the invisible Church, which is fine as far as it goes. But a day is coming when this invisible Church will no longer be invisible at all. And the visible Church (as we have known her) will be a thing of the past.

So instead of seeing two churches at the same point in time and then trying to figure out which one has our allegiance, we need to take the importance of redemptive history into account. For example, if we were told that there were two Peter Smiths, one heavenly and one earthly, we might get confused about which one was the real Peter. But confronted with Peter Smith on Monday and again on Tuesday, we do not have any such problem. In the same way, we should see the visible Church in history growing and developing as all creatures in history do. And we have that same visible Church at the end of history. Under such circumstances, we do not ask which one is the true Church—it is the same Church. Does the Church in history contain those who are not elect? Absolutely. But the Church at the end of history contains all the elect, and none of the nonelect.

[1] The heavenly Church is invisible to me for the same reason the church in China is invisible to me—I am not there to see it.

If someone were to tell me that I had a scriptural duty to honor my mother, I should not respond by asking whether he meant my visible mother or my invisible mother. If he is speaking scripturally, he simply means my mother—as she is today, and as she will be in the resurrection. I honor *her*.

And this is how the Scriptures speaks of this process. The Church is growing up "unto a perfect man" (Eph. 4:13). We are in the process of growing up into Him in all things (Eph. 4:15). When will the process be complete? At the last day, when the Bride is presented to Christ without spot or wrinkle, or any such blemish (Eph. 5:26–27). At the end of history, the eschatological Church will be comprised of all the elect and none of the reprobate. The eschatological Church serves the same *defining* function as the invisible Church, but with one advantage. It is necessarily the same Church that we are members of now, it is a Church grounded in historical reality, and it does not tempt us to think in terms of a Hellenistic upper story and lower story.

Coming back to the text in Hebrews, we are not told that we will *eventually* come to the heavenly Church. The writer says that we *are* come (Heb. 12:22). The Bible does not speak of the Church in heaven, the heavenly Jerusalem, as though it were inaccessible. On the contrary, *we go there every week*. The heavenly Jerusalem is the mother of us all (Gal 4:26)—this is true now, not later. We are able to do this because we are in Christ Jesus. Therefore, in Christian worship on the Lord's Day, through the blood of Christ, we find the reconciliation of all things in heaven and on earth (Col. 1:20). Worshiping in Christ links heaven and earth—how could they be separate now?

How should this affect the way we think? The imperfections now—the spots and wrinkles—do not change the identity of the Bride in the slightest. And no, this is not an encouragement to *be* one of those spots or blemishes, a blemish that will be removed at some point.

Because this language of historical and eschatological differs from the language used by the Westminster Confession, it is appropriate to look at the language of the Confession here. But it is important to note at the outset that this difference is no contradiction at all. The different terminology is suggested because it affirms the same doctrine and is not open to the same objections.

> The catholic or universal Church, which is invisible, consists of the whole number of the elect, that have been, are, or shall be gathered into one, under Christ the Head thereof; and is the spouse, the body, the fullness of Him that filleth all in all. (25:1)

The invisible catholic Church is defined here as the elect, all the chosen from the beginning of the world to the end of it. As the elect, they constitute the body of Christ, His Bride. He is the Head of the Church, and the Church (in this sense) is the fullness of Christ, who is in turn the fullness of everything. Thus defined, there is no immediate problem with affirming that the elect *are* the invisible Church. There are some downstream problems which will be addressed in the following section.

> The visible Church, which is also catholic or universal under the Gospel (not confined to one nation, as before under the law), consists of all those throughout the world that profess the true religion; and of their children: and is the kingdom of the Lord Jesus Christ, the house and family of God, out of which there is no ordinary possibility of salvation. (25:2)

The visible Church is also catholic in an earthly sense, meaning that it is no longer confined to one nation, as it was before under the law. This visible Church is composed of anyone in the world who professes (biblically) to believe the Christian faith. When they make this profession by means of baptism their children are included with them. This visible Church is to be understood as the kingdom of the Lord Jesus. This Church is the household of God, and outside of this Church there is no ordinary possibility of salvation.

And so here is one of the rare places in which we would suggest an improvement on the language of the Confession. A problem is created when we affirm a belief in two Churches *at the same moment in time*, one visible and the other invisible. Are they the same Church or not? If they are, then why are "membership rosters" different? If they are not, then which one is the true Church? We know that Christ has only one Bride. The natural supposition is that the invisible Church, made up of the elect, is the true Church. But this leads to a disparagement of the visible Church, and eventually necessitates, I believe, a baptistic understanding of the Church. Because time and history are not taken into account, we wind up with two Churches on different ontological levels.

It would be better to consider the one Church under a different set of terms, discussed earlier, and which preserve the necessary distinction made by visible and invisible—*historical* and *eschatological*. Because time is taken into account, we preserve the understanding of just one Church, and at the same time preserve the necessary distinction between those Church members who are ultimately saved and those who are ultimately lost. The historical Church is the counterpart to the visible Church, and consists of those throughout history who profess the true faith, together with their children. The eschatological Church is the elect, *but it is not invisible*. At the last day, every true child of God will be there, not one missing, and every false professor will have been removed. At the resurrection of the dead, this Church will be *most* visible.

A second minor problem with the Confession at this point is the assumption that the Jews of the Old Covenant constituted the historical Church, outside of which there was no ordinary possibility of salvation. But the nation of Israel was established to be a priestly nation among the nations. Many thousands outside of Israel were saved during the time of the law. What about Melchizedek, Job, Lot, Jethro, Namaan, the inhabitants of Nineveh who repented under the preaching of Jonah, and those Gentile worshipers for whom Solomon prayed at the dedication of the Temple?

> Unto this catholic visible Church Christ hath given the minis-try, oracles, and ordinances of God, for the gathering and per-fecting of the saints, in this life, to the end of the world: and doth, by His own presence and Spirit, according to His prom-ise, make them effectual thereunto. (25:3)

Within the visible Church, Christ ministers by various means of His appointment. He has granted the ministry of God to the Church, the oracles of God to the Church, and the ordinances of God to the Church. The reason He has done so is so that the saints could be gathered and perfected in the con-text of His household throughout the course of their lives. This Church will remain unto the end of the world, doing this essential work. Christ, through His covenantal presence, and through His Spirit, makes all these gifts effectual to their ap-pointed end. The Lord's Supper is effectual because Christ makes it so. The preaching of the Word is effectual because Christ makes it so.

> This catholic Church hath been sometimes more, sometimes less visible. And particular Churches, which are members thereof, are more or less pure, according as the doctrine of the Gospel is taught and embraced, ordinances administered, and public worship performed more or less purely in them. (25:4)

A perfectionistic approach to the visible or historical Church is not biblical. The catholic, visible Church does not always present the same degree of visibility. And particular Churches, members of the catholic Church, exhibit this same tendency. They are more or less pure, depending on how the gospel is taught and embraced, depending on how the ordinances are practiced, and depending on the purity of worship in their service of God.

> The purest Churches under heaven are subject both to mixture and error; and some have so degenerated, as to become no Churches of Christ, but synagogues of Satan. Nevertheless, there shall be always a Church on earth to worship God according to His will. (25:5)

No perfect Church exists in this fallen world. All churches are prone to error and compromise. This does not necessarily alter their status as genuine churches of Christ. Left unchecked, however, the mixture and error *does* threaten their status as churches of Christ because it is possible for a particular church to degenerate to the point where apostasy occurs. In Romans 11, the apostle Paul warns the Gentile church at Rome that they may fall through covenantal presumption in just the same way that the Jews fell. Particular churches can be removed from the olive tree. However the olive tree itself will always stand.

This is why we can say that there will always be a Church on earth to worship God according to His will. The olive tree will never be chopped down and one day will fill the earth with her fruit. But this does not mean that particular branches cannot be pruned from the tree. This is why we insist that the catholic Church was given a promise that she would never fall. The Church at Rome was given no such promise, and in fact, the dire covenantal warnings mentioned above were delivered expressly to the Church at Rome.

> There is no other head of the Church but the Lord Jesus Christ. Nor can the Pope of Rome, in any sense, be head thereof: *but is that Antichrist, that man of sin, and son of perdition, that exalteth himself, in the Church, against Christ and all that is called God.* (25:6)

The Church cannot have an earthly head, but only the Lord Jesus Christ as Head. This excludes any earthly head, particularly the bishop of Rome. The section in italics, identifying the pope as the Antichrist, has been deleted from a more modern version of the Confession. This improvement involves more than rejecting just an interesting doctrinal understanding of the papacy. This removal opens the way for a preterist understanding of prophecy, over against this particular historicist understanding.

This chapter of the Confession shows that the historic Reformed view was one that held a very high view of the Church. Modern Protestants often do have the low ecclesiology that Rome charged the Reformers with, but in the case of modern Protestantism, the charge is not a slander. In the case of the magisterial Protestant fathers, it is a slander.

> Luther and all the Reformers were conscious that they could be accused of diminishing the Church to a mathematical point, so to speak, and they continually had to defend the evangelical churches against the charge of being merely a *Platonica civitas*, a Platonic state, meaning . . . an ideal Church enjoying a disembodied and illusory existence in the realm of pure abstractions, uncontaminated by the empirical world of space and time, place and history.[2]

At the same time, it is fair to say that for the Reformers the gospel outranked everything. If an apostle or an angel from heaven were to preach an alien gospel, then the true gospel would sit in judgment and the false evangelist would be condemned. But with the recovery of the gospel came the subsequent recovery of the Church. And this is just what we find. "Luther was primarily and passionately concerned for the purity of the gospel: Calvin for the

---

[2] Paul Avis, *The Church in the Theology of the Reformers* (London: Marshall Morgan & Scott, 1981), 4.

purity of the Church—the gospel had already been brought into
the light of day."[3]

Because the gospel is powerful to save people, when that
gospel is recovered it does create some interesting tensions in
the context of the institutional Church.

> The tension which would arise in the development of evan-
> gelical ecclesiology after Luther is prefigured in the combina-
> tion of two distinct concepts in the formula of the Confession .
> . . it is striking that this definition of the Church juxtaposes a
> phrase characteristic of the anabaptistic view of the Church,
> 'congregation of saints' (*congregatio Sanctorum*), and a notion
> more characteristic of the formalism and legalism of the Ro-
> man Church, correct administration of the Word and sacra-
> ments.[4]

The Roman Catholic writer Ronald Knox, normally an astute judge, was far off the mark when he said, "The Ecclesia is
one thing, the Elect are another; and it was the capital mistake of early Protestantism that it never realized that."[5] Actually, the early magisterial Protestants were acutely aware of
this distinction. The anabaptists of course were not, and since
their perspective has come to dominate the evangelical Protestant world, it is not surprising that this misunderstanding is
read back into the time of the Reformation. The tensions between *ecclesia* and *elect* were addressed in the language of
Westminster under the heading of *visible* and *invisible*. We embrace that distinction—but think it needs a better set of
names.

---

[3] Ibid., 13.
[4] Ibid., 25.
[5] Ronald Knox, *The Quotable Knox* (San Francisco: Ignatius Press, 1996), 78.

9

Notae Ecclesiae

In addressing the objectivity of the covenant, at some point we need to come to the questions about the *boundaries* of the covenant. If the covenant is not a category invisible to man, then by what marks are we to know it? Put another way, we have to consider the marks of a true Church. On what scriptural basis do we say that this group is within the covenant, that group outside, and the other group is off sitting in the gray areas?

> But though we, or an angel from heaven, preach any other gospel unto you than that which we have preached unto you, let him be accursed. As we said before, so say I now again, If any man preach any other gospel unto you than that ye have received, let him be accursed. (Gal. 1:8–9)

When God works in history, He is working covenantally in a *sinful* history. In that history, Satan presents himself as an angel of light. Apostles could conceivably fall away and preach a gospel other than the one that Paul preached to the Galatians at the first. Since this is the case, then how are we to navigate? Once converted by the gospel, it is our duty to attach ourselves to the company of the faithful, the congregation of the saints. How do we find them?

Reformation theology is largely dominated by two questions: "How can I obtain a gracious God?" and "Where can I find the true Church?" The two questions are inseparably related and constitute two aspects of the overriding concern of sixteenth-century men with the problem of salvation, for the truth of the old patristic watchword *Nulla salus extra ecclesiam*—no salvation outside the Church—was assumed on all sides.[1]

When God granted the Reformation to the Church, He did so through a glorious recovery of the gospel—preached, poured and eaten. But after the Roman church recovered from the initial shock, they began to ask hard, pointed questions. What are the *notae ecclesiae*—the marks of a true Church? The Reformation had already occurred without such careful scholastic definitions; the Word was unchained and that was enough. The early Reformers simply emphasized a preached gospel, baptism, and the Lord's Supper. A later development added Church discipline, and it is not hard to understand why. A Church with no discipline is a Church with no immune system. Without any discipline, how long will the gospel remain undefiled? How long will the Word continue to be preached without discipline of heretics? How long will the Table of the Lord be undefiled without discipline of libertines?

This was a necessary development, but it still created practical problems. In short order, certain sectarians made "discipline" the center of their theological universe, and they of course disciplined in terms of their own sectarian distinctives. But the sectarians, who became very quick to unchurch others, would have great difficulty with the apostle Paul's "liberalism" (1 Cor. 1:2; Gal. 1:2). The radical sectarians had a thing about discipline. "Here four underlying principles of radical ecclesiology come into view: its voluntarism, its primitivism, its exclusivism, and its obsession with discipline."[2] In contrast, Calvin does not define the *esse* of the Church in terms of discipline. He would agree that discipline is necessary to the

[1] Paul Avis, *The Church*, 1.
[2] Ibid., 55.

bene esse of the Church but would maintain that the question of discipline concerns the periphery, not the center. "Calvin's mature position, however, excludes an appeal to Christian behaviour; it does not make discipline one of the essential marks of the true Church."[3] In other words, lack of discipline will bring about a collapse soon enough but is not to be identified with that collapse.

Taking this a step further, this can be related to the approach taken by the great Anglican, Richard Hooker. "This conviction led Hooker to define the visible Church in a more empirical and pragmatic way than the Reformers—both on the continent and in England—had done, by reference to its outward profession of faith, taken at its face value."[4] While the sectarian overvalued discipline, it appears that the Anglicans undervalued it, and we find ourselves back in Geneva.

We need to ask whether we should seek to find the center or the circumference. The questions that were raised by Rome at that time were about the *boundaries* of the covenant. The Reformation began with a striking emphasis on the *center* of the covenant, which was Christ and Him crucified. But for the early Reformers, this center was not a series of abstractions about Christ (creedal definitions in the sky). Rather, the center was Christ *preached* and Christ given through the sacraments—to be received by faith. The Reformers said that you recognize a man by looking at his *face*, not the ends of his shoelaces, and if you want to recognize the Church, then you must look straight at her Head, who is Christ. As Calvin put it:

> The appearance by which it may be recognized is the question. We place it in the Word of God or (if anyone would so put it), since Christ is her head, we maintain that as a man is recognized by his face, so she is to be beheld in Christ.[5]

[3] Ibid., 33.
[4] Ibid., 71.
[5] Qtd. in ibid., 33.

Calvin's point is a compelling one. "Who of us, to recognize a man, would look at his shoes or his feet?"[6] The Head, Jesus Christ, is recognized by the believer in His gospel and sacraments. The gospel is the center. "On this principle the Reformers were immovable and undivided; it provides the distinctive Reformation concept of the Church . . . one thing is needful; all else is secondary. To save the gospel, all outward forms of order and structure are expendable."[7] But note that this was to save the *gospel*. This did not mean the Reformers thought the historical Church to be unimportant; far from it. Rather, the best thing to do for the historical Church is to get the gospel straight, because it is the gospel that brings the life of the Church.

So the magisterial Reformation rightly emphasized the center, not the edges. This is the miracle of the Word. The Scriptures teach that the gospel creates *life*. And where this life has been created, you have the Church, necessarily connected to her Head.

The seed that brings life is the Word of the kingdom. "But he that received seed into the good ground is he that *heareth the Word*, and *understandeth* it; which also beareth fruit, and bringeth forth, some an hundredfold, some sixty, some thirty" (Mt. 13:23). The seed that brings life is the gospel preached. "Seeing ye have purified your souls in obeying the truth through the Spirit unto unfeigned love of the brethren, see that ye love one another with a pure heart fervently: being born again, not of corruptible seed, *but of incorruptible, by the Word of God*, which liveth and abideth for ever. For all flesh is as grass, and all the glory of man as the flower of grass. The grass withereth, and the flower thereof falleth away: but the Word of the Lord endureth for ever. *And this is the Word which by the gospel is preached unto you*" (1 Pet. 1:22–25). The seed that brings life is the Word of truth. "Of his own will *begat he us with the Word of truth*, that we should be a kind of firstfruits of his creatures" (Jas. 1:18).

[6] Qtd. in ibid., 34.
[7] Ibid., 3.

So the Church consists of those who have been called out of darkness and into the light. We are confident of the objectivity of the covenant, and of the Church, because we are confident *first* of the objectivity and reality and power of the gospel.

This gospel has the power to disturb, perplex—and save. The Reformation did not occur because God raised up some men who were determined to color inside the lines. Pharisees are always tidy-minded and want their religion lined up in orderly little rows. But the kingdom of God is a lot like one description of Luther's sermons—heroic disorder. "Wherein I suffer trouble, as an evil doer, even unto bonds; but the Word of God is not bound" (2 Tim. 2:9). Precisely because the Word is not bound, it is not possible for the *effects* of that Word to be contained. How could it be? Where does new life appear? Wherever the seed has gone.

This is why, in all such matters, the gospel preached outranks wayward archangels, popes, bishops, moderators of general assemblies, senior pastors, world-class theologians, and anyone else who might show up with a different gospel—not that there could be another gospel.

Christ is offered to all of us in the preached Word. Faith is the only thing that can see Him there. Christ is presented to us in baptism and the Lord's Supper. Faith receives Him. If a man has no faith, then all he has is words, water, and a tiny meal—along with all the curses of the covenant. But if a man sees Him by faith, then when he looks around, he is part of the Church.

10

Sacerdotalism

People define *sacerdotalism* differently. For some, it means anyone who uses the word *sacrament*. For others, more accurately, it
means the belief that grace is imparted in a mechanical or magical fashion through the instrumentality of the sacraments. In
other words, the sacraments dispense grace *ex opere operato*,
the way a hot iron burns. But for others, erring more subtly,
sacerdotalism is the view that sacraments do *anything*.

Misunderstanding about what actually constitutes
sacerdotalism is at the heart of the controversy over the objectivity of the covenant. I said earlier that rationalism has made
considerable inroads into the conservative wing of the Reformed faith, and the clear tendency of this rationalism is a re-
ductionistic one. Instead of a robust supernaturalism that applies
to all of life (seen and understood by faith only), the clear tendency of the rationalist system is to disparage the means of
grace. This tendency is seen in B.B. Warfield's book *The Plan of
Salvation*, which is worth quoting on this point at length.

> . . . [I]t has yet been taught in a large portion of the Church (up to to-
> day in the larger portion of the Church), that God in working salva-
> tion does not operate upon the human soul directly but indirectly;
> that is to say, through instrumentalities which he has established as
> the means by which his saving grace is communicated to men. As
> these instrumentalities are committed to human hands for their ad-
> ministration, a human factor is thus intruded between the saving

grace of God and its effective operation in the souls of men; and this human factor indeed, is made the determining factor in salvation. Against this Sacerdotal system, as it is appropriately called, the whole Protestant Church, in all its parts, Lutheran and Reformed, Calvinistic and Arminian, raises its passionate protest. *In the interests of the pure supernaturalism of salvation* it insists that God the Lord himself works by his grace immediately on the souls of men, and has not suspended any man's salvation upon the faithlessness or caprice of his fellows.[1]

In other words, any view that says God uses *any means* to accomplish His purposes in salvation is a corrupted or impure supernaturalism. Of course, objections crowd to mind. What about the preaching of the gospel? Are all the external means that God uses to bring the gospel to lost men a charade? The gospel, missionaries, preaching, baptism, covenant nurture— are all these just a front operation for the *real* work of saving men, which is done by God directly, behind the scenes? What Warfield thought of as "pure supernaturalism" is actually closer to a refried gnosticism, an invisible conduit from God to man, with no contact made with contaminating earthly, incarnational influences. It is telling that in Warfield's famous table illustrating all this, he has the sacerdotalists affirming their views concerning the Church and the "consistent" Calvinists affirming things about the elect.

I quote Warfield at this point knowing that as a confessional Presbyterian he had to (and did) acknowledge that God established and used means of grace within the Church. I do not want to misrepresent him as overtly denying that there are means of grace. But I do want to argue that Warfield was being inconsistent here. I take his insistence that God works "directly" on the human soul as a claim that God is working "apart from means." But elsewhere Warfield acknowledges that God uses such means of grace. But how is this not God working "indirectly?"

[1] B.B. Warfield, *The Plan of Salvation* (Boonton.: Simpson Publishing Co., 1989), 50–51. Emphasis mine.

But whether Warfield's take on this is right or wrong, he claims that it is the universal Protestant view. Is *this* right? Before examining that claim in detail, it must be granted that Protestants have affirmed that the Church with its sacraments are in no sense a ball and chain for Almighty God. "Although it be a great sin to contemn or neglect this ordinance, yet grace and salvation are not so inseparably annexed unto it, as that no person can be regenerated, or saved, without it: or, that all that are baptized are undoubtedly regenerated" (28:5). In other words, the Westminster Confession assumes that grace and salvation are *ordinarily* annexed to water baptism, but, for all that, God remains God and can save when, how, whom He pleases. They are not *inseparably* annexed. Notice in which direction the exception is made. "God *can* save someone apart from baptism, we grant, but that is not what He usually does." Baptism and salvation are not mechanically or magically linked. But in the ordinary course of life, they *are* linked, and we are to speak of them as though they are. And to do so is *not* sacerdotalism.

> Under the gospel, when Christ, the substance, was exhibited, the ordinances in which this covenant is dispensed are the preaching of the Word, and the administration of the sacraments of Baptism and the Lord's Supper: which, though fewer in number, and administered with more simplicity, and less outward glory, yet, in them, it is held forth in more fullness, evidence, and spiritual efficacy, to all nations, both Jews and Gentiles; and is called the new Testament. There are not therefore two covenants of grace, differing in substance, but one and the same, under various dispensations. (7:6)

Under the time of the gospel, this one covenant of grace receives a different administration. The substance of the covenant has come, who is the Lord Jesus Christ, and the ordinances and sacraments are therefore altered—necessarily so. The ordinances of this administration are the preaching of the Word and the administration of the two sacraments.

The things we are called upon to do in this administration are simpler and have "less outward glory." But in the gospel economy the last are first, and this diminution of glory results in greater glory. In the simplicity of Christian worship, the gospel comes in power to all nations, both Jew and Gentile. This manner of worship is called the New Testament. Note that in this section, the Westminster theologians maintain that in the ordinances of the gospel, the covenant is *dispensed*. Not only so, but it is held forth in *spiritual efficacy*. According to Warfield's definition, to have the covenant dispensed in ordinances and to have them be spiritually efficacious, is sacerdotalism. But this is the Westminster Confession, which he claims is anti-sacerdotalist. And so it is, but the inevitable conclusion is that there is something wrong with Warfield's definition.

The division between the covenants does not come between Malachi and Matthew. The two testaments simply describe one and the same covenant of grace. The sin of Pharisaism is not a separate covenant made by God at all, but rather a distortion of the covenant of grace as it was given in the time of the law. God never commanded men to save themselves. He always commands them to come, in sincere faith, to the means He has established. If they do so, they receive blessing through His means. If they come in unbelief, they receive covenant curses. But in all ordinary cases, they are dealing with the means established by God.

> Sacraments are holy signs and seals of the covenant of grace, immediately instituted by God, to represent Christ and His benefits; and to confirm our interest in Him: as also, to put a visible difference between those that belong unto the Church and the rest of the world; and solemnly to engage them to the service of God in Christ, according to His Word. (27:1)

What is a sacrament? A sacrament is a sign, and a sign that *seals* what it signifies. This is not a front operation. The sacraments of the Christian religion therefore are those which signify and seal

the covenant of grace. We know that a practice is such a sacrament if it was instituted by God in order to *represent* Christ
and His salvation. A sacrament is placed upon a particular individual in order *to establish a link* between the promises of the
covenant and that person. A sacrament is also given as a means
of distinguishing the saints of God from those who are not—
to put a visible difference between the Church and the rest of
the world. Now, when God places this visible difference before us, are we not obligated to *see* it? As a result, those with
such a divine mark upon them are obligated by it.

We must also remember in this discussion that sacraments are
inescapable; if we do not accept the two sacraments established in
the Word of God, then we will make up our own. Here, sign this
card. Throw your stick in the fire on the last night of youth camp.

> There is, in every sacrament, a spiritual relation, or sacramental
> union, between the sign and the thing signified: whence it comes
> to pass, that the names and effects of the one are attributed to the
> other. (27:2)

This is something we understand quite well in other realms, and
it is not hard to master. "With this ring, I thee wed." Really? The
water cleanses us and washes our sins away. But only a doofus
would think that water all by itself would wash away sins.
Moderns who are stuck with the language of Westminster want to
say that we actually have to understand this as a *sacramental* union,
with the word *sacramental* being understood as some sort of dilut-
ing agent. But I want to say that it is a sacramental *union*, with
union meaning union. More on this shortly.

> The grace which is exhibited in or by the sacraments rightly used,
> is not conferred by any power in them; neither doth the efficacy of
> a sacrament depend upon the piety or intention of him that doth
> administer it: but upon the work of the Spirit, and the word of

institution, which contains, together with a precept authorizing the use thereof, a promise of benefit to worthy receivers. (27:3)

There is no power in the sacrament itself; there *is* power in that which the sacrament is identified with—the blessings and curses of the covenant itself. This being the case, the sacrament does not depend for its efficacy on the godliness of the one administering the sacrament. Suppose a pastor runs off with the church organist the week after someone's baptism. Does that nullify the baptism? Not at all. The applications of the sacraments are *objective*, meaning that the Spirit is at work in the words of institution. This is what brings about the resultant blessings (or curses), as covenant members are faithful or faithless.

> There be only two sacraments ordained by Christ our Lord in the Gospel; that is to say, Baptism, and the Supper of the Lord: neither of which may be dispensed by any, but by a minister of the Word lawfully ordained. (27:4)

As opposed to the teaching of Rome, there are not seven sacraments, but only two—baptism and the Lord's Supper. According to the Confession, they are to be administered by lawfully ordained ministers of the Word. This is a good idea for reasons of good government, but I do not believe it should be a confessional issue. What should be a confessional issue is that the rulers of the Church are responsible to see to it that a right understanding of the sacraments is to be preserved, and so, at the very least, they should oversee and approve all occasions where the sacraments are dispensed.

> The sacraments of the old testament, in regard of the spiritual things thereby signified and exhibited, were, for substance, the same with those of the new. (27:5)

The New Testament era did not usher in new sacramental realities—the people of God have always had the sacramental realities of initiation and nurture. What changed was the visible nature of the signs, not the constant reality of the things signified. Now, with this in mind, we see that Warfield's definition is lacking and that it certainly does not represent the historic Protestant position. Ronald Wallace summarizes Calvin's view. "One important function of the sacraments is to confirm and seal the Word. Though the sacraments are ineffective without the Word, nevertheless the bare word cannot have its full effect without the sacraments."[2]

But how is it possible to see the sacraments as efficacious, which the Protestant fathers certainly did, but at the same time recognize that they have no magical power in themselves? We must not think of ourselves as empty receptacles and the sacraments as filled decanters, full of spiritual juice, which are then poured into us. Rather than seeing the question of the sacraments as this kind of an ontological and metaphysical question, we have to see it as a *covenantal and relational* question. We are persons and we are communing with God, who is tri-personal, and we do so in the sacraments. *They are therefore performative acts.* A man might say the words "I do" a million times during the course of his life, but when he says them in a church in front of witnesses with his bride across from him, the words are a performative act, and they change everything.

Grace is not a fluid that can fill up a reservoir. Grace is a covenantal relationship between persons. Now the Scriptures do tell us that grace can be both added and multiplied. "Grace and peace be multiplied unto you through the knowledge of God, and of Jesus our Lord" (2 Pet. 1:2; cf. 1 Pet. 1:2; Rom. 1:7). But we have to be careful not to fall prey to abstract nouns. If I pray that someone's marital happiness will increase,

[2] Ronald Wallace, *Calvin's Doctrine of the Word and Sacrament* (Eugene: Wipf and Stock, 1982), 137.

I am asking that a relationship between persons will flourish and not that something will happen in their marital "tank," something that can be checked with a dipstick.

But for a number of historical reasons, many evangelicals (in the grip of individualism) have come to believe, to use Steve Wilkins' illustration, that grace is an invisible substance that flows to each individual Christian through an invisible hose as though we were all spiritual deep sea divers with the hose on our helmets running up to heaven.

They believe that the receipt of grace has conditions, but no means down here on earth. To believe that there are actual means of grace is thought to encourage superstition. But this is not a scriptural assumption, nor is it the historic Protestant conviction. Further, as we have discovered, this conditions/ means distinction has not discouraged superstition, but rather has just created a new set of superstitions—without any biblical basis.

The grace of God is so abundant that we cannot hope to itemize all the different ways He pours out grace upon us. But we can note some of the central means of grace. We know that we are blessed by grace through faith—but where does faith look? Can God's grace be seen? "Who, when he came, and had seen the grace of God, was glad, and exhorted them all, that with purpose of heart they would cleave unto the Lord" (Acts 11:23). What Barnabas saw was relations between persons. Grace is ministered to us through horizontal means—and we can see those means which God in heaven uses to bestow grace upon us.

What are some of the means which God uses to bless us in this way? First, we are urged to have grace, by which we may worship rightly (Heb. 12:28–29). Grace is evident in preaching (Eph. 3:8) and as a result of preaching (Acts 4:33; 1 Cor. 15:10–11). Another obvious means of grace is baptism—we were saved, not by our own works, but by the washing of regeneration and renewal by the Holy Spirit (Tit. 3:4–6). The result of this is that we are justified by His grace (v. 7). The Lord's Supper is another important means—we are to be established by eating grace, not Jewish sacrifices (Heb. 13:9). We have an altar from which they cannot eat (v. 10). We are to offer up the sacrifice of praise and thanksgiving (v.15). We are to do good and are to take care that we do not forget to communicate (*koinonia*; v. 16). This partaking or *koinonia* is what occurs in the Supper (1 Cor. 10:16). Unbelief tries to detach these activities from other persons, but the objectivity of the covenant means that this can never be successfully done.

Music is another vehicle of grace—we are commanded to sing psalms, hymns and spiritual songs *to one another* with grace in our hearts (Col. 3:16). Body life is yet another—we have manifold gifts which are to be exercised toward *one another* as stewards of grace (1 Pet. 4:10). Grace is not limited to the Lord's Day, as we see when we consider godly conversation. Day to day conversation with *one another* is to be a ministry of grace (Eph. 4:29). Feasting is still another means of grace. As we learn how to eat and drink at the Table, we learn to feast everywhere else by grace (1 Cor. 10:30–31).

Because grace is objective and presented to us in so many different ways, it can easily be despised, which is what covenant breakers do. How is grace despised? Scripture says we can receive grace in vain (2 Cor. 6:1). We can fall from grace (Gal. 5:4). This is obviously not talking about efficacious, heavenly grace, which we cannot fall away from. It is talking about the grace that is present in the worship service of the local church. When such individuals fall away, they do so because of a refusal to be humble. "God resisteth the proud, and giveth grace to the humble" (1 Pet. 5:5). A proud man looks down his nose with contempt at the means offered to him through the ministry of the Church. Another problem is hypocrisy. "Grace be with all them that love our Lord Jesus Christ in sincerity.

Amen" (Eph. 6:24). Another grace-disrupter is bitterness—
take care "lest any man fail of the grace of God; lest any root
of bitterness" spring up (Heb. 12:15).

In our day when the doctrines of sovereign grace are so
much despised, we have to be warned of the dangers of all
forms of self-salvation—note the emphases. "Of how much
sorer punishment, suppose ye, shall he be thought worthy,
who hath trodden under foot the Son of God, and hath counted
the blood of the covenant, wherewith he was sanctified, an
unholy thing, and hath done despite unto the Spirit of grace?"
(Heb. 10:29)

Having said all of this, and while resisting Warfield's pro-
posed solution, there are two senses in which we do not describe grace toward us as mediated. First, grace is shown to us
before the world was made, before we were made, before any
of the means of grace were even created. "Who hath saved us,
and called us with an holy calling, not according to our works,
but according to his own purpose and grace, which was given
us in Christ Jesus before the world began, but is now made
manifest by the appearing of our Saviour Jesus Christ, who
hath abolished death, and hath brought life and immortality to
light through the gospel" (2 Tim. 1:9–10). But this is clearly a
statement about God's ultimate intentions. God doesn't use
means here because the means are not created, but this is not
unmediated salvation for us either, because neither were we
created.

Second, on the basis of His elective decree before all
worlds, God commands the light of the gospel to shine in our
hearts (2 Cor. 4:6). The gospel here is mediated. But the actual shining is the efficacious result of God fulfilling His promise by giving true faith—a real mystery (Rom. 11:5). God
creates the saving light to shine just as He did in the first creation—*ex nihilo*. Two men hear the gospel preached and only
one responds. The difference between them is not a difference

in the means, but rather in the fact that God decreed that the means would be efficacious in one instance and not in the other. This decree is not independent of means because it is a decree concerning those means.

In all this, we are to think of grace. We are to *stand* in it. "By whom also we have access by faith into *this grace wherein we stand*, and rejoice in hope of the glory of God" (Rom. 5:2). We are to grow in this grace. "But *grow in grace*, and in the knowledge of our Lord and Saviour Jesus Christ" (2 Pet. 3:18). And lastly, we are to be strong in it. "Thou therefore, my son, *be strong in the grace* that is in Christ Jesus" (2 Tim. 2:1).

If grace is a covenant relationship between persons for blessing, and if sacraments are performative acts, Peter Leithart makes it clear that there are more than the two options of "evangelical" immediacy or sacerdotalism.

> In criticizing Warfield on these points, I am not affirming a "sacerdotal" view of salvation, but suggesting that the antithesis between sacerdotal and evangelical is a false one that a Trinitarian account of sacraments (and salvation) will help us to escape.[3]

The word *trinitarian* here refers to the ultimate *covenantal and personal context* of all sacramental acts. "Thus, a Trinitarian framework leads to a strong affirmation of baptismal efficacy that is as far as possible from anything 'magical' or 'sacerdotal.'"[4]

In the presence of God, all our sacramental acts are performative acts. God has established the meaning of these acts, and so that is what the action in context means. This is different from saying that the sacraments mean something the way a detached label means something else. The baptismal water is simply water—until it is applied in such a way that

---

[3] Peter Leithart, "'Framing' Sacramental Theology: Trinity and Symbol," *Westminster Theological Journal* 62 (2000): 5.

[4] Ibid., 15.

makes the action a performative, covenantal act. The bread and wine are simply bread and wine. This is why Peter Leithart notes "that there is no 'eating as such' but only 'eating in this or that way.'"[5]

This understanding of the sacraments as events in the history of covenant relationships makes it possible for us to give an account of false partakers. "A dissembling member is not a 'social' Christian but a 'false son' or 'unfruitful branch,' and this is a theological fact with eternal consequences."[6]

A true son is brought into the covenant and is nourished there. A false son is brought into the covenant and by his unbelief incurs the chastisements of that covenant. Objectively, both the true and false son are brought into the same relation. But because one of them is elect and the other not, the former is faithful and the latter is faithless. "Objectively, baptism makes me a member of Christ's body, and this becomes an episode in the story of who I am."[7] It is an episode in the story of who I am regardless of my faith or lack of it.

> A baptized man can renounce Christ, turn persecutor of the Church, reject everything he once confessed, forget his baptism. Having once passed through the waters, however, his every action thereafter, including those that are wholly inconsistent with his baptismal identity, are actions of a baptized man.[8]

Put another way, there is no such thing as a merely nominal Christian any more than we can find a man who is a nominal husband. There are many faithless husbands, but if a man is a husband at all, then he is as much a husband as a faithful one. He is a covenant breaker, but this is not the same as saying that he has no covenant to break. In the same way, there are multitudes of faithless Christians, who do not believe what God said at their

[5] Peter Leithart, "Modernity and the 'Merely Social,'" *Pro Ecclesia* 9, no. 3: 323.
[6] Ibid., 325.
[7] Ibid., 326.

baptism. But the tragedy is that there are many conscientious conservative Christians who do not believe what God said at their baptism either.

> This is the "new life" effected by the "waters of regeneration." These are "merely social" facts only if one assumes that this house is not really God's house and this Table not really his Table. But that, of course, is simple unbelief.[9]

So there are no nominal Christians, but there are wicked and faithless Christians. These faithless Christians incur the displeasure of God because they trample underfoot the blood of the covenant by which they were sanctified. And this brings out one feature of historic reformed thought on this subject which requires further development and qualification.

> The sacramental problem is that Calvin consistently denies that the non-elect really receive what the sacraments signify, though he is equally insistent that, within the covenant, what the sacrament signify [sic] is genuinely offered.[10]

There is no need to contradict what Calvin taught here, but it does require an additional qualification. What we need to say is that the nonelect do not receive what the sacraments signify *for blessing*. They do taste and participate, and they taste Christ as their covenant Lord and Judge. They do come in contact with the blood of the covenant, but this happens because they have trampled it.

If the sacraments are thought of as *covenant actions between persons*, rather than as static, ontological realities contained within the font or resting on the Table, we do two things. We avoid the swamp-like superstitions of true sacerdotalism, as well as the arid rationalism that detaches all of our actions from what they are meant to *seal* for us.

[8] Ibid., 326.
[9] Ibid., 330.
[10] S. Joel Garver, "John Calvin on Apostasy" in *TAS*.

11

Baptism Now Saves

Our previous understanding of the sacraments will be a great help to us as we come to consider the two sacraments in particular. We have noted repeatedly that baptism in water is objective, and it establishes an objective covenant relationship with the Lord of the covenant, Jesus Christ. Of course this baptism does *not* automatically save the one baptized; there is no magical cleansing power in the water. We reject the Roman Catholic notion that saving grace goes in when the water goes on. We deny any *ex opere operato* efficacy to the waters of baptism. We also deny the modern Protestant reductionism that says that when the water goes on, somebody gets wet.

In one sense, it is true that if you baptize an unrepentant pagan, you get a wet pagan. But it is the thesis of this book that far more happens than this. When you baptize an unrepentant pagan, what you actually get is a covenant-breaker. His baptism now obligates him to live a life of repentance, love and trust, which he is refusing to do.

As we have said, baptism therefore accomplishes something, in much the same way that the simple words *I do* accomplish something at a wedding. But what? And how does the Bible actually speak of baptism? The answer is disconcerting to many within the evangelical tradition.

The like figure whereunto even baptism doth also now save us
(not the putting away of the filth of the flesh, but the answer of
a good conscience toward God), by the resurrection of Jesus
Christ. (1 Pet. 3:18–22)

Before discussing this in detail, lest anyone get nervous, no
man was ever put right with God by walking through some
ritual observance, biblical or otherwise. Evangelicals are *rightly*
afraid that some might come to believe the words of the Nicene
Creed in a wooden and superstitious fashion—"one baptism for
the remission of sins." Many millions have sinned in just this way.
But since the Nicene Creed is part of the confession of faith
shared by all the churches in my presbytery, how should *I* take
this phrase? A good place to start our interpreting is with
phrases in the Bible that say essentially the same thing. How do
we handle *them*?

When the Scriptures speak of water baptism, what kind of
language is commonly used? A good place to begin is with the
text quoted earlier. Water baptism now saves us. Peter tells us
that baptism saves, and his subsequent qualifier does not mean
that baptism does not save. He is not taking away with one hand
what he has given with the other. It means that baptism saves
in this fashion, but not in that fashion.

Baptism does not save by means of the water (not putting
away physical dirt), but baptism does save by the resurrection of
Jesus Christ accompanied by the answer of a good conscience.
This reference to a removal of physical dirt is likely not addressing those who thought that their morning shower washed away
their sins, but rather addressed certain aspects of the Jewish ceremonial. In order to be ceremonially clean for worship in the
Temple, Jews had to get physically clean, using lots of water. The
ashes of a heifer, for example, cleansed the worshipers so that
they were outwardly clean (Heb. 9:13). In this sense, Christian
baptism does more fully and efficaciously what the ordinances of
Old Covenant washing also did in a limited way.

When Peter was preaching the first sermon of the New Covenant era, his message cut his listeners to the heart. They cried out, "What should we do?" How many of us would give Peter's answer? "Then Peter said unto them, Repent, and be baptized every one of you in the name of Jesus Christ for the remission of sins, and ye shall receive the gift of the Holy Ghost" (Acts 2:38). This is where the phrase in the Nicene Creed came from—baptism for the remission of sins.

When Saul was first converted, Ananias knew just what was called for and apparently did not adequately guard against superstition in his language. "And now why tarriest thou? arise, and *be baptized, and wash away thy sins*, calling on the name of the Lord" (Acts 22:16). In blunt language, Ananias told Saul to come to the baptismal font in order to wash away his sins.

The Bible also speaks of the washing of regeneration. The word for *washing* in Titus 3:5 is literally *laver*: "Not by works of righteousness which we have done, but according to his mercy he saved us, by the washing of regeneration, and renewing of the Holy Ghost." We find the reality referred to in Ephesians 5:26. This is one of the few places where the Bible refers to regeneration, and it is the only place where it does so in reference to the conversion of individuals. In doing this, Paul speaks of the *font* of regeneration.

When Jesus tells His apostles to preach the gospel throughout the world, He teaches them what the response to that gospel needs to be. "He that believeth and is baptized shall be saved; but he that believeth not shall be damned" (Mk. 16:16).

All this seems to be pretty plain. What are we to do with this? Are we Roman Catholics yet? For the historically astute, the answer is *of course not*. But it has to be confessed that the biblical response to these things (and the historic Reformed formulation of them) looks Roman Catholic to many modern evangelicals. But this is because they are heirs of the radical Anabaptist reformation, and not of the magisterial Reformation. We have gotten to such a low point in our awareness of our heritage that a man can be thought to be quoting Roman Catholic formulae when he is actually quoting that old papist, John Knox.

The Westminster Confession sheds light on this question for us. "There is, in every sacrament, a spiritual relation, or sacramental union, between the sign and the thing signified: whence it comes to pass, that the names and effects of the one are attributed to the other" (27:2). There is a sacramental *union* between consecrated bread and the body of Jesus Christ. There is a spiritual *relation* between the wine and the Lord's blood. This sacramental union is so tight that it is fully appropriate to refer to one reality in terms of the other.

Return for a moment to the illustration of marriage. Does anyone really stumble over the words "with this *ring* I thee wed"? Does anyone really think that a little piece of metal contains such awesome powers? Not at all—there is a sign and the thing signified, and there is in performative acts a covenant *union* between the two. This means that, and, in a real covenantal sense, this *is* that.

Confusion over such things is not a new problem. Moses tells the people of God to circumcise their hearts (Deut. 10:16). Joel says they are to rend their hearts and not their garments (2:13). Paul tells us that the true Jew is the one circumcised in the heart by the Spirit (Rom. 2:29). Go and find out the difference between mercy and sacrifice, Jesus said.

Consequently, the analogy of faith requires us to say that water baptism without saving faith is worse than useless. The bare formalist attempts to bring about a divorce between sign and thing signified is guilty of a very great sin. What God has joined together no man should dare to separate.

But a similar warning must go to the devotional pietist, the one who would be wiser in his speech than God has chosen to be in His holy Word. *He also wants a divorce* between sign and thing signified. He says we must never say that baptism saves or washes away sin, because blockhead believers will always get the wrong idea and think they can go to Heaven by taking a bath.

We must not be children in our thinking but grow up into sacramental maturity. This maturity requires that we submit to the wisdom of God. And God is the one who has given us the water through which genuine faith may see a glorious forgiveness. As those who would be historic Protestants, this means facing what they actually taught, and not what we assumed them to have taught.

> Baptism is a sacrament of the new testament, ordained by Jesus Christ, not only for the solemn admission of the party baptized into the visible Church; but also to be unto him a sign and seal of the covenant of grace, of his ingrafting into Christ, of regeneration, of remission of sins, and of his giving up unto God, through Jesus Christ, to walk in the newness of life. Which sacrament is, by Christ's own appointment, to be continued in His Church until the end of the world. (28:1)

Raise your hand if you knew that the Westminster Confession taught baptismal regeneration—but more on this in a moment. We have discussed sacraments generally; we now come to discuss the two sacraments specifically, in turn. Baptism is one of the sacraments of the new covenant. It was ordained by Jesus Christ as a sacrament in the words of the Great Commission. He told His disciples that the mark of His disciples was to be baptism. Disciple the nations, He said, *baptizing* them. The signification of baptism is twofold, that is, it points in two directions. The first is the solemn recognition that the one baptized has been admitted into the historical Church of Christ. At the same time, the baptism also points *away* from the person, to the objective meanings of baptism. Baptism means that the one baptized has a sign and seal of the covenant of grace, the one baptized has been grafted into Christ, he has the sign and seal of regeneration, forgiveness of sins, and the obligation to walk in newness of life. This sacrament is perpetual in history.

Baptism is given in order to be *to the one baptized* "a sign and seal of the covenant of grace, of *his* ingrafting into Christ, of *regeneration*, of remission of sins." A sacerdotalist understanding of this would require Arminianism—true conversion followed by true apostasy. On the other hand, reductionist rationalism has to reject this portion of the Confession or pretend that it is not there.

Of course there are baptized covenant members who are not individually regenerate. They are the ones who reject what God is offering to them in their baptism. They therefore fall away from the *covenant* and not from election.

> Not only those that do actually profess faith in and obedience unto Christ, but also the infants of one, or both, believing parents, are to be baptized. (28:4)

No disagreement exists among Christians over the propriety of baptizing pagans upon their profession of faith in Christ, along with their expressed willingness to follow and obey Him. But in addition to their baptisms, their infants (or dependent children) are also to be baptized. This is the case even where only one of the parents is converted. It should be obvious that this process helps set us up for the problem we are considering. To bring people into the Church "wholesale" this way creates the highly visible problem of covenant members who are covenant breakers. Our Baptist brothers have sought to avoid this by requiring a profession of faith from each individual before baptizing them, but this just gets us into the same dilemma via a different route. In the Bible Belt, it is not uncommon for the deacons in Baptist churches to perform a sweep operation through the Sunday School classes to ensure that everyone makes a profession of faith around the age of ten. They go forward, get baptized, and remain a good Christian until they get their driver's license. From this, we should recognize that the purity of the Church is actually guarded by disciplining in terms of our baptisms and not by withholding baptisms. Covenant breaking is a common problem in *all* Christian communions. This is why the New Testament teaches us so much on how to deal with it.

> Although it be a great sin to contemn or neglect this ordinance, yet grace and salvation are not so inseparably annexed unto it, as that no person can be regenerated, or saved, without it: or, that all that are baptized are undoubtedly regenerated. (28:5)

Neglect of baptism is a great sin but not an unforgivable one. We are to consider baptism and regeneration together, but we are not to treat this as an absolute. In other words, some who are not baptized will be saved, and not all who are baptized are saved. But as discussed earlier, while we do not take the connection between water baptism and grace and salvation as an absolute, we do take it as the norm.

> The efficacy of Baptism is not tied to that moment of time wherein it is administered; yet, notwithstanding, by the right use of this ordinance, the grace promised is not only offered, but really exhibited, and conferred, by the Holy Ghost, to such (whether of age or infants) as that grace belongeth unto, according to the counsel of God's own will, in His appointed time. (28:6)

Contrary to Warfield, baptism is efficacious. But the efficacy of the sacrament is not tied to the moment when it is administered. By means of baptism, this efficacious grace is *conferred* on the elect at the appropriate time, the time of conversion, and it is *the applied grace of their baptism.*

This being the case, baptism is not to be administered over and over. If it were only efficacious based on the timing of it, then in certain cases, it would have to be administered again. But fortunately, it is not. To administer baptism again is therefore to deny that the first baptism was a Christian baptism. And this is why the "sacrament of Baptism is but once to be administered unto any person" (28:7).

It is crucial to reiterate that this is a matter of covenant relationship and not a matter of priestcraft. We do as we are told and do not try to peer into the secret things (Deut. 29:29).

> This covenantal act of baptism brings the person into a conditional relationship with God. Individual election is unconditional; but individual election is part of the secret decretal will of God, no "list" of elect individuals having been revealed.[1]

Baptism is visible and therefore accessible to us. "Every baptized person objectively enters into covenant with Christ, just as every man and woman who weds, objectively enters into the marriage covenant."[2] No one assumes that every husband will automatically have a successful marriage. Nor should we assume that every Christian will go to Heaven. But all husbands are in fact married.

We therefore receive all baptized individuals as covenant members. "[Y]et it must be emphasized, that until the Church acts to formally remove someone from the covenant by way of excommunication, all baptized persons are to be considered full covenant members."[3] When we do this in the case of covenant breakers, we are treating their baptisms with greater respect than they do. The typical evangelical response to "nominal" Christians, however, allows the covenant breaker to feel some sense of moral superiority—"How can you say my baptism is worthless? I may not be a very good Roman Catholic, but at least . . ." But we are saying that baptism provides the faithful

---

[1] Randy Booth, "Covenantal Antithesis" in *The Standard Bearer: A Festschrift for Greg Bahnsen*, ed. by Steve Schlissel (Nagadoches: Covenant Media Press, 2002), 40.
[2] Ibid., 45.

covenant member with means to exhort disobedient Christians in terms of their baptism: "Why do you despise your baptism the way you do?"

When we do this, we are spared the indignity of turning the scriptural language on its head. Peter Leithart chides Karl Barth for this. "For Barth, when the writer says, 'bodies washed with pure water', he means that what are not really bodies are not really washed by what is not really water."[4]

There is an apostolic succession in the Church, but it is not a succession delivered through ordination. Rather, it is a succession of baptisms, which have fulfilled the Old Testament type of priestly ordination.

> To draw near, one must come under blood and water—a comparatively rare combination in Levitical law but found in the ordination rite (Exod. 29:4,21; Lev. 8:6,30). Hebrews 10:22 describes baptism with imagery borrowed from ordination.[5]

And again, "I argue that Heb. 10:19–22 states precisely that baptism confers priestly privileges."[6]

The fact that the new covenant is a spiritual covenant does not mean that it is an ethereal covenant. "As much as the first, the second covenant is concerned with bodies—with Jesus' bodily self-offering and with the bodily consecration and living sacrifice of his people."[7]

This consecration really happens. God really does it. His people are genuinely set apart; a visible difference is placed between them and the world. By means of baptism, baptism with *water*, grace and salvation are conferred on the elect.

---

[3] Ibid., 48.

[4] Peter Leithart, "Womb of the World: Baptism and Priesthood of the New Covenant in Hebrews 10:19–22," *Journal for the Study of the New Testament* Vol.78 (2000): 52.

[5] Ibid., 54.

12

The Lord's Supper

Given the history of sacramental controversy and the fact that eucharistic idolatries have not been rare in Church history, many Christians have trouble with any hint of sacerdotal monkeyshines when it comes to the Lord's Table. This is understandable, but it has created its own set of problems.

> Our Lord Jesus, in the night wherein He was betrayed, instituted the sacrament of His body and blood, called the Lord's Supper, to be observed in His Church, unto the end of the world, for the perpetual remembrance of the sacrifice of Himself in His death, the sealing all benefits thereof unto true believers, their spiritual nourishment and growth in Him, their further engagement in and to all duties which they owe unto Him; and, to be a bond and pledge of their communion with Him, and with each other, as members of His mystical body. (29:1)

The Lord Jesus established this sacrament the night He was betrayed, and the sacrament is very rich in meaning. It is to be commemorated in the Church until the end of the world. For most evangelicals, the Supper is limited to the first meaning mentioned here—the understanding is accurate as far as it goes, but does not go very far. But the import of the Supper goes far beyond a mere memorial to us. In fact, the Supper as memorial also means that it is presented to God as a memorial, a reminder. Just as the rainbow was a memorial to God, so the Lord's Supper reminds Him to forgive us our sins. Some might object to this saying that God does not need reminders. This is quite true, but it is also true that because He is God He doesn't need Christians telling Him what not to do. *He* tells us to remind Him, which is why we do.

The Lord's Supper is first a memorial of Christ's self-sacrifice; secondly, a sealing of all the benefits of Christ's death unto true believers; third, a spiritual nourishment of all true believers who partake; fourth, a covenant renewal on the part of those who partake; fifth, a bond from Him of the fact that He is our God and we are His people; and sixth, it is communion with our fellow believers, fellow members of the body of Christ.

The language of the Confession is very strong, and it is utterly inconsistent with the Warfieldian view that saving grace is not mediated. By this means, all the benefits of Christ's death are *sealed* in true believers. True believers are nourished. They renew covenant with God. God makes promises to us in the Supper. And we are enabled to discern the Lord's body in one another. With regard to this last point, Peter Leithart explains how this Calvinist view of the Supper is thoroughly Augustinian.

> Similarly, in *De Doctrina Christiana*, Augustine treats signs to an unprecedented extent within the context of a theory of communication, such that signs are a means by which one passes on the motions of his soul to another. While this concept has an overly intellectualistic cast, it moves in the direction of a sociological view of signs (which is at the same time a theological view) by emphasizing their role in interpersonal relations. And this enters his explicit sacramental theology: Augustine insists that Christ is in the *res* of the sacraments, but the Christ who is such is the *totus Christus* of Head and Body.[†]

[†] Peter Leithart, "Conjugating the Rites: Old and New in Augustine's Theory of Signs," *Calvin Theological Journal* 34 (1999): 146.

We see Christ in the sacrament, but we do this in the same
way and at the same time that we see Christ in our brother.
Those who fight and squabble with Christian brothers are not
discerning the body.

But these wonderful things do not occur in the Lord's Supper because magic tricks are being done on the altar.

> In this sacrament, Christ is not offered up to His Father; nor
> any real sacrifice made at all, for remission of sins of the quick
> or dead; but only a commemoration of that one offering up of
> Himself, by Himself, upon the cross, once for all: and a spiri-
> tual oblation of all possible praise unto God, for the same: so
> that the popish sacrifice of the mass (as they call it) is most
> abominably injurious to Christ's one, only sacrifice, the alone
> propitiation for all the sins of His elect. (29:2)

As far as the issue of sacrifice is concerned, the Supper is no real
sacrifice but only a sacramental commemoration. But to say it is
a commemoration *sacrificially* does not mean that it is only a
commemoration in other respects, those already mentioned.
Christ is not sacrificed to the Father in the Supper. The Supper
does involve "all possible praise" for the sacrifice Christ offered,
but this is not the same as a sacrifice proper. The doctrine of the
perpetual sacrifice in the Mass is therefore injurious and insult-
ing to the once for all death of Christ on the cross for sins.

> The Lord Jesus hath, in this ordinance, appointed His ministers
> to declare His Word of institution to the people; to pray, and
> bless the elements of bread and wine, and thereby to set them
> apart from a common to an holy use; and to take and break the
> bread, to take the cup, and (they communicating also them-
> selves) to give both to the communicants; but to none who are
> not then present in the congregation. (29:3)

What are the constituent elements of the Supper? What does it
take for the Supper to be held? The minister needs to declare the

words of institution, showing his authorization to hold the Supper; he should pray; he should bless the bread and wine so that they are sanctified; he should break the bread; he should take the cup; he should distribute both to the communicants; and his distribution should be limited to those who *are present.*

> Private masses, or receiving this sacrament by a priest, or any other, alone; as likewise, the denial of the cup to the people, worshipping the elements, the lifting them up, or carrying them about, for adoration, and the reserving them for any pretended religious use; are all contrary to the nature of this sacrament, and to the institution of Christ. (29:4)

Distortions of the Supper include these features: private communion, denial of the cup to the people, worshiping the elements, acting in such a way as to provoke the worship of them, and setting them aside for other religious use. In this we see that our fathers were concerned to preserve the Supper as a covenantal meal. They were very concerned lest the meal turn into something else. The action of eating in the presence of God, together with His people, is central.

> The outward elements in this sacrament, duly set apart to the uses ordained by Christ, have such relation to Him crucified, as that, truly, yet sacramentally only, they are sometimes called by the name of the things they represent, to wit, the body and blood of Christ; albeit, in substance and nature, they still remain truly and only bread and wine, as they were before. (29:5)

The outward elements are not transformed in their physical nature by any act of consecration. They *truly* become the body and blood of Christ *sacramentally*, not physically. The elements in themselves remain bread and wine.

> That doctrine which maintains a change of the substance of
> bread and wine, into the substance of Christ's body and blood
> (commonly called transubstantiation) by consecration of a
> priest, or by any other way, is repugnant, not to Scripture
> alone, but even to common sense, and reason; overthroweth
> the nature of the sacrament, and hath been, and is, the cause of
> manifold superstitions; yea, of gross idolatries. (29:6)

The doctrine of transubstantiation is contrary to Scripture.
Not only so, but it is also contrary to common sense and reason. It maketh no sense. The error is not a trivial one because
it overthrows the very nature of a sacrament, and stumbles
the people of God into superstition and idolatry.

> Worthy receivers, outwardly partaking of the visible elements,
> in this sacrament, do then also, inwardly by faith, really and in-
> deed, yet not carnally and corporally but spiritually, receive
> and feed upon, Christ crucified, and all benefits of His death:
> the body and blood of Christ being then, not corporally or car-
> nally, in, with, or under the bread and wine; yet, as really, but
> spiritually, present to the faith of believers in that ordinance, as
> the elements themselves are to their outward senses. (29:7)

Having said all this, having qualified against the dangers of
idolatry, those who partake of the sacrament worthily really feed
upon Christ. *The Westminster Confession teaches that there is a real
presence of Christ's body and blood in the act of faithful eating at His
Table.* But in order to truly feed upon Christ, it is not necessary
for the bread and wine to be changed. We feed upon Christ by
faith (which is not the same as saying we pretend to feed upon
Him). We feed spiritually through the bread and wine presented
to our outward senses. Christ is presented to us in the sacrament. We see Him there *by faith*, and not by sight. Christ presents Himself to the faith of believers in the same manner that
the physical elements present themselves to our hands and
mouths.

Although ignorant and wicked men receive the outward elements in this sacrament; yet, they receive not the thing signified thereby; but, by their unworthy coming thereunto, are guilty of the body and blood of the Lord, to their own damnation. Wherefore, all ignorant and ungodly persons, as they are unfit to enjoy communion with Him, so are they unworthy of the Lord's table; and cannot, without great sin against Christ, while they remain such, partake of these holy mysteries, or be admitted thereunto. (29:8)

According to the Confession, two types of men should be kept from the Supper—the ignorant and the wicked. When they do partake, they do not receive what is signified. We have already mentioned that this is one place where the historic Reformed position could use some refinement. It is what Joel Garver said was the "sacramental problem" in the Calvinist position. If this chapter is taken as meaning that unworthy partakers do not receive the *blessing* promised to any right use of the Supper, then this is correct. But if it means that the wicked do not partake of Christ *in any sense* when they partake of the Supper, then I think this is wrong. The curses of the covenant fall upon wicked and ignorant partakers precisely because they defile the body and blood of the Lord. The reason they are guilty of the body and blood of the Lord is because they came to it in an unworthy way. When this happens, they eat and drink to their own damnation. They cannot defile what they did not receive. The contrast that Scripture presents at the Table is blessings and *curses*, not blessings and no blessings.

With regard to the "ignorant," we also want to be careful how we fence the Table here. There are types and degrees of ignorance. For example, there are ignorant people who ought not to be, and so they should be excluded from the Table because their ignorance is culpable. But a five-year-old is necessarily ignorant and, to some extent, so is a mature Christian. We are all *ignorati*, but the Supper is given to nourish and strengthen us, as was seen in an earlier section. Consequently, we do not want to be maneuvered into saying that Christians should grow big and strong, and then we will give them some food. This aspect of the Confession has to be carefully considered when discussing the issue of child communion, although I do not believe it excludes child communion necessarily. It seems clear that the ignorance addressed (at least here) is a culpable, stiff-necked ignorance, and is not the ignorance which every worthy partaker of the Supper confesses daily.

13

Church Unity

What does all this do to the vexed problem of Church unity? In one way, it makes the problem far easier to understand. But in another way, this can provoke a crisis of courage—acting on what we know could cause great problems and threaten our ungodly denominational system.

> With all lowliness and meekness, with longsuffering, forbearing one another in love; endeavouring to keep the unity of the Spirit in the bond of peace. There is one body, and one Spirit, even as ye are called in one hope of your calling; One Lord, one faith, one baptism, One God and Father of all, who is above all, and through all, and in you all. (Eph. 4:2–6)

We find three basic points in this text. The first is that the unity of the Spirit is something to be kept. It is not manufactured by us, but rather is to be preserved by us. The second thing is the attitude which is willing to obey this command, and which rejoices in it. This is the attitude of lowliness, meekness, patience and loving forbearance. It follows that the attitudes that defy this word from God would be haughtiness, insolence, impatience, and harshness. The third thing is the nature and basis of the unity that is to be kept. This given unity (one body) is grounded in the fact that everything about the Christian faith has trinitarian unity—one Spirit, one hope, one Lord, one faith, one baptism, and one God and Father of all.

What are some of the ways in which we have come to believe that it is our duty to disregard this duty of preserving
the unity of the Spirit in the bond of peace?

One of the first answers that should come to mind is that of
denominations. Now in some ways, denominations are a necessary evil. When the sheep are scattered, one of the sheep cannot
simply stand up and "unscatter" them all. But what we can do is
refuse to acknowledge that our current state is anything other
than a disgrace. Why then form another presbytery, as the
church I pastor helped do a few years ago? The answer of
course is that we were, prior to that time, an independent
congregation, and every independent congregation is simply a
small denomination. When we joined together with two other
independent churches, we were giving the broader Christian
Church a net loss of two denominations. Everything we do
should be striving in the direction of unity.

Some think that striving for unity means refusal to fight over
anything, which is not at all correct. We need to have far
more Church fights over some things and far fewer over others. We should have more fights over pastors adopting openness theism and fewer fights over what color to paint the
church nursery.

And when we fight over false teaching in the pulpit, we have
to remember that to say that a certain man is not qualified to
teach the Word is not the same thing as saying he is not a Christian. Put another way, defrocking is not excommunication. We
need to define from the Scriptures the standards of leadership
(which means raising the standard, and fighting more) and also
define from the Scriptures the standards of fellowship (which
means broadening the standard, and fighting less). Our central
concern in our fight for reformation involves who ascends to the
pulpit and not who ascends to heaven.

As we consider the issues surrounding Church unity, we have
to reject the notion of voluntarism. We have somehow come to

believe that denominations are defined by themselves and not by Christ. But this is as much a failure of faith on our part as anything else. But any Christian church is nothing more and nothing less than what Jesus Christ says about it. For example, if the Scripture teaches election then this is the "position" of all churches in principle, regardless of what their denominational documents might say about it. This means that children of Baptists are in the covenant anyway, Nazarenes are eternally secure, and charismatics are not exercising the gift of prophecy.

As we debate issues that divide Christian churches from one another, we have to take care we do not adopt ungodly definitions of love. We have assumed that love is to be defined by Hallmark cards rather than by the Word of God. Take the typical modern evangelical assumption about love, and then ask yourself if there is a contradiction here. "I would they were even cut off which trouble you. For, brethren, ye have been called unto liberty; only use not liberty for an occasion to the flesh, but by love serve one another. For all the law is fulfilled in one word, even in this; Thou shalt love thy neighbour as thyself" (Gal. 5:12–14). In verse 12, Paul wishes the Judaizers would overachieve and cut the whole thing off. In the next verse, he says the Galatians are to serve one another in love. In the next verse, he quotes the second greatest commandment. And in verse 15, he tells them not to bite and devour one another. Apparently, his comment in verse 12 was not an example of such biting and devouring.

A comparable example would be a pastor, who, in a debate with a sectarian group that insisted that baptism through immersion by their church was necessary for salvation, said that he wished someone would baptize them all until they bubbled. Is that *nice*? Maybe not, but it is biblical. And it would not be hypocritical for such a pastor to call for Church unity and covenant love in the next breath. This is because Scripture is our authority and not our own sentimentalism.

As we proceed to practical application, we need to guard against some of our faulty assumptions listed above. One of the most important areas of application is in the matter of receiving baptism. Paul says that we are one, and he says so because we have one Lord, one faith, and one baptism. This has enormous practical ramifications.

Some baptisms in history needed to be repeated, and at the culmination of redemptive history, they all came together in Christian baptism. We can call these "baptisms fulfilled." At a unique time in history, those who faithfully partook of the ceremonial washings of the old covenant were thereby prepared for Christian baptism (Acts 2:38; 19:3–4). But the transition still required a final baptism, into the name of the Father, Son and Holy Spirit.

Other baptisms from outside the Christian faith should never be received, but rather denied. A religious washing in the Ganges should not be accepted as "a baptism" (Mt. 28:18–20). Unbelieving nations still need to be baptized. This kind of thing is happening outside the covenant altogether. In such cases, baptisms are not really "denied" but rather are declared to have been no baptisms at all. We should also encourage this in cases of gross apostasy—e.g., Mormonism or the Jehovah's Witnesses. Given the trinitarian nature of our text, any anti-Nicene (not *ante*-Nicene) baptisms should be considered outside the pale.

When we are dealing with corrupt churches (as opposed to apostate churches), our response should be to restore their baptisms. We should have learned that covenantal living involves blessings and *curses*. This means that "receiving baptisms" is not the same thing as "approving of baptisms." Paul tells us, for example, that observance of a sacrament can do more harm than good (1 Cor. 11:17). We must therefore distinguish "validity of baptism" from "efficacy of baptism *for blessing*." Trinitarian baptisms can still be corrupted baptisms—e.g., Church of Christ,

Roman Catholic, or liberal Protestant baptisms. They are to be received in order to be nursed back to health.

Then, in the vast majority of cases, we should find Christian churches gladly receiving or accepting one another's baptisms. There are many other Christian groups with whom we may strive for like-mindedness together (Rom. 15:5; Phil. 2:2). Under such circumstances, we are to receive such baptisms routinely and joyfully.

Striving for unity is not the same thing as striving to build a big tent. Christian unity is not a lowest common denominator affair. The *more* we emphasize God's worship, attributes, truth, loveliness, and goodness, the more true unity emerges.

Part III

Apostasy and Assurance

14

Blessed Assurance

We are commanded in Scripture to make our calling and election sure (2 Pet. 1:10). This is not a grievous command; being confident in God's salvation is a wonderful frame of mind. God does not want His children to lack an assurance of their standing before Him; He wants us to *know* what He has given to us. This is a command that can actually be obeyed. "These things have I written unto you that believe on the name of the Son of God; that ye may *know* that ye have eternal life and that ye may believe on the name of the Son of God" (1 Jn. 5:13).

Those who believe on the name of Christ are invited to know the nature of their inheritance—which is eternal life. But if we have learned that apostasy is a real sin, committed by real covenant members, then what can be the basis of our assurance? And can anyone have assurance without presumption? In 2 Corinthians 13:5, Paul says, "Examine yourselves, whether ye be in the faith; prove your own selves. Know ye not your own selves, how that Jesus Christ is in you, except ye be reprobates?"

The Scriptures require self-examination. But as we should also have learned, the Word prohibits morbid introspection. What is the difference? Self-examination holds up the mirror of the Word and asks honest questions. Morbid introspection holds up the mirror of self and spews forth doubts. But doubts, in the form of *"What if . . ."* cannot be answered in principle. *Questions* always have an answer in principle; doubts are framed in such a way as to exclude answers. With this said, what does the Bible teach on this? What are the marks of one who makes his calling and election sure?

A Christian assured of his salvation is *holding fast to Jesus Christ*—"That if thou shalt confess with thy mouth the Lord Jesus, and shalt believe in thine heart that God hath raised him from the dead, thou shalt be saved" (Rom. 10:9). The lordship of Christ is confessed with the mouth, and God's declaration of the lordship of Christ in the resurrection (Rom. 1:4) is believed in the heart. "Whosoever shall confess that Jesus is the Son of God, God dwelleth in him, and he in God" (1 Jn. 4:15; cf., Jn. 5:24). An honest confession of who Jesus is—the Son of God—means that God dwells in the one who made the good confession. He has made this confession because he is holding fast to Christ.

A Christian assured of his salvation has *the gift of the Spirit*—"Hereby know we that we dwell in him, and he in us, because he hath given us of his Spirit" (1 Jn. 4:13). Those who are saved enjoy a mutual indwelling. We dwell in God, and God dwells in us. We know this is the case because the Spirit is given to us. The Bible teaches this in multiple places. "For ye have not received the spirit of bondage again to fear; but ye have received the Spirit of adoption, whereby we cry, Abba, Father. The Spirit itself beareth witness with our spirit, that we are the children of God" (Rom. 8:15–16; Gal. 4:6–7). The context of Romans shows that the Spirit leads us in putting to death the misdeeds of the body, but His presence in our lives is unmistakable. Scripture teaches that the Holy Spirit is an earnest payment (Eph. 1:13–14; 2 Cor. 5:5–6). In other words, one who has received this earnest payment, guaranteeing their final inheritance, has a profound assurance indeed. If they fall away this means that God did not keep His guarantee. And if God did not keep His guarantee, then He forfeits the earnest payment. This means that if one of the elect, a regenerate man, quickened by the Holy Spirit, were to fall away

and go to Hell, the Holy Spirit would have to go with him—
which of course is absurd. Therefore, he cannot fall away.

Because these things are true, we can always say that "hope
maketh not ashamed; because the love of God is shed abroad in
our hearts by the Holy Ghost which is given unto us" (Rom.
5:5).

A Christian assured of his salvation has *love for the brothers*—
"We know that we have passed from death unto life, because we
love the brethren. He that loveth not his brother abideth in
death" (1 Jn. 3:14). A man who is baptized, but who hates his
brother, is demonstrating by that hatred that he is not truly living
in life. He has not *genuinely* passed from death to life. Conversely,
someone who does not love has not passed out of death. "A new
commandment I give unto you, That ye love one another; as I
have loved you, that ye also love one another. By this shall all
men know that ye are my disciples, if ye have love one to another" (Jn. 13:34–35).

A Christian assured of his salvation has true *humility of
mind*—"And said, Verily I say unto you, Except ye be converted,
and become as little children, ye shall not enter into the kingdom of heaven" (Mt.18:3). We have to be careful here because
in many instances we get this turned around. We say that little
children have to become like adults before they can enter the
kingdom. They have to meet with the elders before they can
come to the Table, and often preparation for communion
seems more like preparation for ordination. We say children
must become like adults; Jesus said adults have to become like
children. To do this requires humility of mind, which is a gift
of the Holy Spirit.

A Christian assured of his salvation has *delight in the means of
grace*—"As newborn babes, desire the sincere milk of the Word,
that ye may grow thereby: If so be ye have tasted that the Lord is
gracious" (1 Pet. 2:2–3). God gave my wife and me three children.
We did not have to teach any of them how to cry for milk

because they were all born hungry. It is the same with the new birth. Spiritual infants are born hungry. They want the things of God. "How amiable are thy tabernacles, O LORD of hosts! My soul longeth, yea, even fainteth for the courts of the LORD: my heart and my flesh crieth out for the living God" (Ps. 84:1–2, 10). When someone is genuinely converted, it is not necessary to chase him down the street in order to get him to seek out spiritual food. Those converted on the day of Pentecost under Peter's preaching devoted themselves to the apostolic discipline, continuing steadfastly in it (Acts 2:42). This is because the "law of thy mouth is better unto me than thousands of gold and silver" (Ps. 119:72). A mark of real conversion is delight in the means of grace.

A Christian assured of his salvation *understands spiritual things*—"For the preaching of the cross is to them that perish foolishness; but unto us which are saved it is the power of God" (1 Cor. 1:18). The unconverted heart can make nothing out of the ways of God. "But the natural man receiveth not the things of the Spirit of God: for they are foolishness unto him: neither can he know them, because they are spiritually discerned" (1 Cor. 2:14). How many of us have had this experience? Before we were converted, the Scriptures were just a bunch of religious God-words. When God turned our hearts, the Bible suddenly turned into English.

A Christian assured of his salvation is *obedient*—"And hereby we do know that we know him, if we keep his commandments" (1 Jn. 2:3). Note that this does not say that we do not know Him if we sin in a particular instance. It says, rather, that we know that we have come to know Him if we are obedient. Walking in obedience is necessary for a biblical assurance of salvation. A backslider can obviously be a saved individual, but nothing is more unbecoming than a backslider who boasts in his assurance. He might be right, but he is not pointing to biblical criteria.

We see the same thing in Romans: "For if ye live after the flesh, ye shall die: but if ye through the Spirit do mortify the deeds of the body, ye shall live. For as many as are led by the Spirit of God, they are the sons of God" (Rom. 8:13–14). The Holy Spirit leads those who are truly converted, and He leads them in mortifying the misdeeds of the flesh.

Ongoing defeat by the world is not consistent with scriptural assurance of salvation. "For whatsoever is born of God overcometh the world: and this is the victory that overcometh the world, even our faith. Who is he that overcometh the world, but he that believeth that Jesus is the Son of God?" (1 Jn. 5:4–5). As J.C. Ryle once put it, the converted man is "no longer like a dead fish floating with the stream of earthly opinion."

A Christian assured of his salvation is *chastened for disobedience*—lest anyone take the previous item in a perfectionistic way, saying that true Christians can never sin, the Bible teaches us what happens to the genuinely converted when they *do* sin.

> And ye have forgotten the exhortation which speaketh unto you as unto children, My son, despise not thou the chastening of the Lord, nor faint when thou art rebuked of him: For whom the Lord loveth he chasteneth, and scourgeth every son whom he receiveth. If ye endure chastening, God dealeth with you as with sons; for what son is he whom the father chasteneth not? But if ye be without chastisement, whereof all are partakers, then are ye bastards, and not sons. (Heb. 12:5–8)

When we sin, God disciplines us by removing our joy (Gal. 4:15; Ps. 51:12). He does not let us continue in our sin and in good fellowship with Him at the same time.

So in reviewing these scriptural criteria of assurance, remember that the point is not to cudgel yourself in their name and on their behalf. The point is to look at yourself in the mirror and then to go away remembering what you look like

(Jas. 1:23–24). And in the remembering, recall by faith that you look like Jesus Christ.

Objective assurance is found in real faith responding to an objective gospel. Objective assurance is never found through trying to peer into the secret counsels of God, or into the murky recesses of one's own heart. The gospel is preached, the water was applied, the Table is now set. Do you believe? The question is a simple one.

A faithful Christian looks to his baptism for assurance, but he needs to see more there than just water. The Word always accompanies the sacrament. And so a Christian searching for biblical assurance should take these passages of Scripture, see how they are all fulfilled in the font and Table, and then rest in his salvation.

15

Apostasy: A Real Sin

We have seen that nothing happens in the salvation (or damnation) of anyone that comes as a surprise to God. As we seek to understand the *reality* of apostasy, we must not do so in a way that makes God a helpless savior—wanting desperately to save us but still unable. Nor may we address it in a way that troubles God's people needlessly.

Every Christian who reads his Bible knows of those passages which make it look as though someone can lose their salvation.

> For it is impossible for those who were once enlightened, and have tasted of the heavenly gift, and were made partakers of the Holy Ghost, and have tasted the good Word of God, and the powers of the world to come, if they shall fall away, to renew them again...(Heb. 6:1–9)

Every Reformed Christian has had to study how to answer his Arminian friends who produce such passages in any debate over the perseverance of the saints. What are we to make of such things?

Before getting to the root of the matter, first a caution. Those who tend to melancholy and morbid introspection need to take great care here. The temptation will be to tremble at the things that should make you glad and to be encouraged by things that should make you tremble. In the previous chapter we saw a *biblical* approach to assurance of salvation—which God intends for His people. The warnings are in Scripture for a reason, but that reason was *not* so that tender consciences would be troubled.

Apostasy is a real sin in real time. It is important for us to settle in our minds at the outset what an apostate falls away *from*. In shorthand, he falls away from Christ; he falls from grace (Gal. 5:4). But what does this mean? In the text quoted above, he has been *enlightened* (an early Church expression for baptism), he has *tasted* the heavenly gift, he has been made a *partaker* of the Holy Spirit, and so on. There is a certain kind of reality to this experience that is assumed. The cut-away branch has no fruit (which is why it was cut away)—but it has had sap (which is why it had to be cut away).

The Arminian errs by making such a person soundly converted at the beginning, only to undo it through his own choices later. In the Arminian scheme such a person was identical to one who perseveres in every respect, but then through his own bad choices, he undoes it all. This is obviously at odds with what the Scriptures teach about the sovereignty of God in our salvation.

But the Reformed have their own set of problems here. One such problem is to assume that all such warnings are hypothetical. In other words, God warns His elect away from something that cannot happen to them—something like erecting a giant "BEWARE OF THE CLIFF" sign in the middle of Kansas. The fundamental problem with treating the passages as hypothetical is that the *reality* of the warning is often assumed in the warning. Demas really did fall away. Unbelieving Jews were really cut out of the olive tree and the Gentiles were warned that the same thing could happen to them. Judas fell away. These are not hypothetical warnings.

Another Reformed exegetical problem is to err by making such a person disconnected from Christ (in every respect) from the beginning. The Bible does not permit this option either. The Arminian needs to hear the Words of Christ: "Depart from me; I *never* knew you"—in other words, something was wrong from the start. The Reformed need to hear some other Words of Christ: "If a man abide not in me, he is cast forth as a branch." The one cast out as a branch *was a branch*, and not some bit of tumbleweed caught in the branches. So there is such a thing as genuine covenantal connection to Christ which is not salvific at the last day. Far from helping a little bit, having had such a connection makes things far worse for them. "For if after they have escaped the pollutions of the world through the knowledge of the Lord and Saviour Jesus Christ, they are again entangled therein, and overcome, *the latter end is worse with them than the beginning*" (2 Pet. 2:20). The curses of the new covenant are terrible indeed. The pictures given of this in Scripture are uniform and consistent at this point.

A common (and erroneous) assumption is that the new covenant contains nothing but automatic blessings. It is assumed that the covenant of grace (in its ethereal heavenly guise) can do nothing but save. But this is not what the Bible teaches. Covenant members in the new covenant are judged more severely than the covenant members of the old were. "*Of how much sorer punishment*, suppose ye, shall he be thought worthy, who hath trodden under foot the Son of God, and hath counted the blood of the covenant, wherewith he was sanctified, an unholy thing, and hath done despite unto the Spirit of grace?" (Heb. 10:26–29). It is simply false to assume that the old covenant had blessings and curses, while the new has nothing but blessings. Both are covenants, and so both have blessings and curses. The new covenant is a far greater covenant, and this means that the blessings are much greater and the curses far more dreadful.

Unbelieving olive branches are cut out of the olive tree in the new covenant era. The warning is by no means a hypothetical one. "Boast not against the branches. But if thou boast, thou bearest not the root, but the root thee. . . .Because of unbelief they were broken off, and thou standest by faith. Be not highminded, but fear: For if God spared not the natural branches, take heed lest he also spare not thee" (Rom. 11:18–21).

Fruitless branches on the Vine of Christ are cut away. "If a man abide not in me, he is cast forth as a branch, and is withered; and men gather them, and cast them into the fire, and they are burned" (Jn. 15:1–6). There is no way to read the New Testament without simply concluding that this really happens.

God gives great and precious promises. The elect believe them. God tells His children to look to *Him* for salvation. Those who do are saved. Those who obligate themselves under the terms of the covenant law to live by faith but who then defiantly refuse to believe are cut away.

Now God is not trying to trick us into believing we are saved when we are not. The sin of apostasy is real, but it is also flagrant. The sin of apostasy is real, but those who torment themselves over this should save their breath for walking uphill.

Nonelect covenant members who look to themselves for their salvation receive great condemnation. They receive this condemnation because they are covenant breakers. But breaking covenant occurs because of *unbelief*, lack of faith, and because of lack of good works. One problem in our contemporary debate is caused by those who assume that if we say the new covenant can even *have* covenant breakers, then these covenant breakers must have failed through lack of works. But when Paul tells the Roman Christians that they could fall away just like the Jews, he also tells them *why* that would happen. They fell because of unbelief, and you stand by faith. Of course, when there is a lack of faith there is also a lack of works. And when a living faith is present, so are the good works which God prepared beforehand for us to do (Eph. 2:10).

Elect covenant members who are tempted to look inside themselves for assurance will only find doubts (and to their surprise later, eternal life). Elect covenant members who look to Christ on the cross and Christ on the throne in evangelical faith receive assurance and life (1 Jn. 5:13). But the covenant breakers who fall away do so because they have denied, in its robust historical sense, *sola fide.*

All this is consistent with the teaching of the Westminster Confession.

> Nevertheless, they may, through the temptations of Satan and of the world, the prevalence of corruption remaining in them, and the neglect of the means of their preservation, fall into grievous sins; and, for a time, continue therein: whereby they incur God's displeasure, and grieve His Holy Spirit, come to be deprived of some measure of their graces and comforts, have their hearts hardened, and their consciences wounded; hurt and scandalize others, and bring temporal judgments upon themselves. (17:3)

All is not sunshine. The elect may stumble and fall, and many of them do. Because of external temptations from Satan and the world, and internal corruptions like lust and laziness, the elect may fall into gross sin. Further, they may continue in their rebellion for a time. During such times, they bring down on their own heads the displeasure of God and the grief of the Holy Spirit. They cannot continue to enjoy the blessings associated with the Christian faith while in such a state. They have their comforts and graces taken from them. They find themselves hardened for a time. They wound their own consciences, which means that their consciences cannot function as they ought to. They hurt others in the faith, and they set themselves up for temporal chastisement. They, being elect, are not vulnerable to *eternal* punishment, but the discipline meted out in this life can be severe. They neglect the means of their preservation for a time, and so they fall into spiritual trouble. Nonelect covenant members neglect the means of their preservation in a more fundamental sense, which is why they fall away.

It is important to note that the doctrine of preservation applies to the elect, not to all and sundry covenant members.
Both are equally in the covenant, and both have means of
preservation near at hand. The elect may neglect them, but
only for a time. The nonelect neglect them at a profound
level.

> The grace of faith, whereby the elect are enabled to believe to
> the saving of their souls, is the work of the Spirit of Christ in
> their hearts, and is ordinarily wrought by the ministry of the
> Word, by which also, and by the administration of the sacra-
> ments, and prayer, it is increased and strengthened. (14:1)

The ordinary course of events is this: the Word is preached,
and God uses that Word to transform a sinner's heart by the
agency of the Holy Spirit. As a result of this transformed heart,
the elect are enabled to believe to the saving of their souls. If
they could have repented and believed with their old heart, they
didn't need a new one. But once this transformation is complete, the Word and resultant faith *do not disappear*. The Word,
along with baptism, the Lord's Supper, and prayer, works to increase and strengthen the faith of the believer, the same faith
which was the instrument used to justify him. The work following conversion has much in common with the work of conversion. It springs from the same source. As God uses our faith as
the instrument of justification and sanctification, so also does
He use means to nourish that faith and keep us persevering.
God uses second causes, and even within the sacramental
bounds of the Church, God works with these second causes,
either necessarily, freely, or *contingently*.

> Although, in relation to the foreknowledge and decree of
> God, the first Cause, all things come to pass immutably, and
> infallibly; yet, by the same providence, He ordereth them to

fall out, according to the nature of second causes, either necessarily, freely, or contingently. (5:2)

God upholds everything. He directs everything; He dis-
poses and governs every creature, every action, and every
thing that is. This is something He does, whether the creature
in question is a cluster of galaxies, or a cluster of atoms. The
hairs of our head are numbered. This He does in holiness and
wisdom. His providence (for this is what we call it) is according to a foreknowledge that cannot be shown to be in error,
which in turn is based on His free and unalterable counsel. The
reason He does this is so that His wisdom, power, justice,
goodness, and mercy might be glorified. It follows that we
should not whisper this doctrine of providential care, or keep
silent about it, for fear that it might not glorify Him. Our
fears for His glory are nothing compared to His zeal for His
glory.

But this relates to perseverance, backsliding, and apostasy.
His providence determines that all things will come to pass; the
end is known and cannot be changed. But that same providence
also knows what will happen causally the moment before. God
oversees the end, but also the means. And His providence of the
means is fully consistent with the nature of secondary causes—
some things happen necessarily, like a rock tumbling in an ava-
lanche. Other things happen freely, as when a man chooses to go
left instead of right. Other things happen contingently, as when
one thing depends upon another. Chori Seraiah notes the importance of this in questions of apostasy. "This does not mean that
God is surprised by our actions; by no means. It means that this
is how we see things played out in the providential fulfilling of
the decrees of God. The means by which men apostatize from
the covenant is unfaithfulness. The means by which men persevere in the covenant is faithfulness."[1] In other words, to assert

[1] Chori Seraiah, "The God of Contingencies," (<http://www.cmfnow.com/
RPCUS/seraiah.html>.)

that men fall away because their salvation was contingent upon
continued faithfulness in the gospel is not to deny the sovereignty of God at all.

> God, in His ordinary providence, maketh use of means, yet is
> free to work without, above, and against them, at His pleasure.
> (5:3)

The fact that we have asserted that God uses means does not
mean that we hold He is *bound* to use means. This would be to
deny Him the power to work miracles. He is the Lord, and He
does as He pleases. Ordinarily, a pastor who sees someone falling
away from the faith sees a pattern that countless pastors before
have seen. God uses these contingent means.

We do not see the covenant from God's vantage point. We
see from "underneath," and this means that we accept what
God says about all covenant members, and we accept what He
says about the distinction between covenant members.

> The problem of covenant breakers within the ranks of cov-
> enant members can only be solved by understanding the ob-
> jective nature of the covenant while allowing for distinctions
> within the covenant.[2]

Apostasy reveals something about the ultimate destinations
of individuals because it is part of the historical process that
God uses to get us there. So we have to consider the covenant
in two ways. Joel Garver points to the necessity of this, as
well as the problem with it.

> Now, as a shadow cast by this picture, we can, of course, say
> that there is a sense in which those who persevere were spe-
> cially (or individually) elect and those who were elect for a

---

[2] Booth, 31.

time were only covenantally (or generally) elect (to use Calvin's language for a moment). *And that's not an unwarranted theological conclusion.* But that's not the way the Scriptures generally speak, I think, and it is precisely in our "covenantal" election that "special" election is realized and made known. Thus, we should not drive a wedge between "special" and "covenantal" elections, for special election simply is covenantal election for those, who by God's sovereign electing grace, persevere. For those who fall away, covenantal election devolves into reprobation.[3]

The Corinthians had begun to believe that they were really something—did they not have baptism and the Lord's Supper? But Paul interrupts them, somewhat abruptly, in order to remind them that the Jews had just the same things. They were baptized into Moses in the cloud and in the sea. They too had a spiritual meal, and spiritual drink. And their bodies were scattered over the desert. Drinking Christ will not automatically keep you from judgment. At Corinth, it was the *reason* for judgment.

Paul presents this to us in 1 Corinthians 10 as an example and warning (1 Cor. 10:6–11). Just as Israel had been baptized into Moses in the cloud and the sea and all were made to drink the same spiritual drink (10:1–4), so also, by one Spirit we are all baptized into one Body and are made to drink one Spirit (12:13; the prooftexts of the Westminster Confession of Faith apply this text to the visible Church; XXV.ii.)[4]

We like to pretend that the New Testament is filled with *automatic* covenant blessings, but the only way to maintain this illusion is to come up with an invisible covenant that no one can point to in such a way as to prove us wrong. We like to pretend that this is

---

[3] S. Joel Garver, "A Brief Catechesis on Covenant and Baptism" (<http://www.lasalle.edu/~garver/cateches.htm>). Emphasis mine.

[4] S. Joel Garver, "Scriptural Indications" in *TAS*.

a point of distinction between the old and the new covenants, whereas in fact it is one of the places where the New Testament draws *parallels*, with solemn warning. In this respect, the New Testament church was no different than the church of Jews in the wilderness. Jews in the wilderness apostatized; Christians in the first century apostatized. Much of the New Testament was written with this concern front and center.

> The entire New Testament, and this is especially clear in the epistles, is written to a covenant community composed of both the elect and the non-elect. Nevertheless, the New Testament consistently addresses those who respond to the covenant promises (elect and non-elect alike) as "brothers," "sisters," "sons," "forgiven," "chosen," "children of God," and so on.[5]

The fact that the first-century churches had nonelect members did not keep the biblical writers from addressing them in terms that meant full salvation. This is because we are to let God be true though every man be a liar. The problem is not a difficult one to understand. But it is sometimes hard to reconcile it with some of our more recent traditions.

> Thus the Scriptures sometimes speak of these nonelect in terms that, strictly and properly speaking, characterize a true and full state of salvation. In his eternal purposes in election, however, God does not grant these individuals to partake of the fullness of salvation in Christ—if they were to do so, they would not fall away.[6]

---

[5] Ibid.
[6] Ibid.

16
Heretics and the Covenant

In a time teeming with heresies, we have no shortage of wrong responses to heresy. This is because an arch-heresy underlies many orthodox responses to more obvious heresy, the arch-heresy of individualism. Because of this, we have allowed ourselves to be maneuvered into a place where we are forced to make a false choice between unity and purity. In order to avoid this error, we must be like Timothy, who was told to "study to shew thyself approved unto God, a workman that needeth not to be ashamed, rightly dividing the Word of truth" (2 Tim. 2:15–21).

So what problem is created by the heretic? For instance, we have some who reason that since these *other* fellows (liberals, etc.) are certainly part of the visible Church, then our relationship with them should be collegial. In other words, we should schmooze with one another all the way down Aaron's beard. Others reason that "If that lesbian bishop is a Christian, then I'm a Hottentot." Since they are clearly not Christians, except in name, the only appropriate response is to go the individualistic route and "come out from among her and be ye separate."

But the problem here is that it is hard to find the brakes. We soon find ourselves members of the church of just one, and we are starting to have doubts about him. The first option undervalues the importance of covenant-keeping. The second undervalues the importance of covenant membership. There is a third way.

We must receive everyone who is lawfully baptized in the name of the Father, Son, and Holy Ghost as a fellow Christian. This means that they are counted as a member of the covenant, which is not the same thing as saying they are faithful to it. But this is a fallen world, and we must note that to say that someone is "a husband" is not necessarily a compliment—it may be the grounds for the accusation against him. In other words, certain fellow Christians are to be considered our mortal enemies. When someone breaks covenant in our midst, we have more choices than two—that of leaving to form our own splinter group, or staying in order to join in the debauchery.

So what does the Bible say about heresy in our midst?

First, the Bible teaches that *heresy reveals faithfulness*—God sends heresies to test us, to find out what is really in our hearts (1 Cor. 11:17–20; Deut. 13:3). We learn here that heresies are rebellion and that they serve to help manifest those who are approved by God, or, put another way, to identify those who have not joined in the rebellion and who are resisting it.

Secondly, we should note that *heresy is obvious*. There are some who have a hard time finding it—scholars, scribblers, and other scribes, but to most believers, heresy is obvious. "Now the works of the flesh are *manifest*" (Gal. 5:19–21). One of the works of the flesh that follow in this list is the work of sectarian heresy. Here we also see that God will punish the heretic. But for our purposes here, we should note that the sheep don't have to go to graduate school to find out the difference between a shepherd and a wolf. Heresy is obvious— denying the deity of Christ, the substitutionary atonement, or that God knows the future. These are not difficult questions.

In the third place, *heresy is sectarian*—"For I know this, that after my departing shall grievous wolves enter in among you, not sparing the flock. Also of your own selves shall men arise, speaking perverse things, to draw away disciples after them" (Acts 20:29–30). Such men want a following they can call their *own*.

In order to get them, heretics have to make a distinction between what they are saying and what faithful ministers say. Heretics speak perverse things for two reasons—one is that as enemies of God they hate His truth, and the other is that there is no other way to split off a segment of the flock for themselves. So heresy is sectarian. A warning is in order here. This does not mean that a sectarian cannot be orthodox, for he can be, but we should still be most careful about the sin of schism. Sectarians are in peculiar danger because lack of accountability is never good.

In the fourth place, *heresy falls headlong*—despite the swift destruction it brings, heresies can still be popular (2 Pet. 2:1–2). And while Peter says that heretics bring on themselves *swift* destruction, he does not say how this comes about.

What are we to do about it? It is no sin against charity to identify the problem. According to Scripture, *heretics are to be identified*—the congregation at Rome is told to mark or identify men who cause divisions and who offend against the doctrine received (Rom. 16:17–18). They are to be marked so that they might be *avoided*. The identification is related to this avoidance. *Heretics are to be rejected*—Titus is told to "reject" a heretic after one and two admonitions (Tit. 3: 9–11). The language of one and two indicates some sort of formal discipline. But reject as what? A teacher? A communicant? My understanding is that this injunction is given to Titus in his role as an apostolic emissary, overseeing the installation of pastors and elders. They are rejected, in the first instance, from positions of teaching and preaching. None of this is to be done in a panic because *heresy is useful*—"But in a great house there are not only vessels of gold and of silver, but also of wood and of earth; and some to honour, and some to dishonour. If a man therefore purge himself from these, he shall be a vessel unto honour, sanctified, and meet for the master's use, and prepared unto every good work" (2 Tim. 2:15–21). Paul's illustration here is telling. A great house—

which is what the house of the covenant is—contains many different kinds of vessels. We have everything there—the exquisite vase of an Athanasius in the entryway, the solid mahoghany book rack of a John Calvin, the solid silver jewelry case of an Anselm. But off in the bedrooms, we have the chamber pots of Pelagianism, and back in the kitchen we find the battered aluminum can of openness theism full of potato peelings, which some think constitutes the solution to the problem of evil. This is what it means to have a great mansion, and so we should remember the limited usefulness of heresy, when kept in its dumpster-bound place.

As noted earlier, the best illustration of how we should understand the center of this is found in marriage. Mark this well: *adultery is not the same thing as divorce.* It is certainly covenantal unfaithfulness and is grounds for divorce, but if there is no divorce, then the marriage remains binding on both parties. An adulterous husband is a covenant-*breaking* husband, not an *ex*-husband. In short, we must distinguish covenant-*breaking* from covenant-*separation.*

Suppose a husband was being notoriously promiscuous. Would we say, well, at least he's *married*? At least he's a *husband*? If a liberal bishop says that Jesus is not God, do we say, well, at least the bishop is a Christian? It is quite true that the bishop is a Christian, which is what makes his infidelity so horrendous.

How do our two earlier rejected positions—separatism and compromise—deal with such an illustration? The separatists would say such a person is not really a husband at all, in *any* sense of the word. But in that case, he is not committing adultery. When some cleric denies every article in the Apostles' Creed, is he breaking any vows? Is he breaking covenant with God? The separatist has to say *no*. But the schmoozers are no better. They would say that since he is a husband (after all) his sexual indiscretions must be tolerated, and perhaps debated at the next meeting of the theological society. In contrast to both, faithful covenant-keepers would say that he is an unfaithful husband, or, to fulfill the illustration, a wicked Christian. To allow (in terms of theology, not discipline) that the Church contains such evil men is to think in terms of the Church, and not in terms of the Sect.

> Melancthon was not moving in the direction of the gathered Church of the Anabaptists and separatists . . . he was not legislating for a sect-type but a church-type of Christianity . . . And in the *Apology* Melancthon had commented: "We concede that in this life hypocrites and evil men are mingled with the Church and are members of the Church according to the outward associations of the Church's marks—that is, Word, confession and sacraments—especially if they have not been excommunicated." Here the Reformers availed themselves of the old scholastic distinction between the Church "properly speaking" (*ecclesia proprie dicta*) and the Church "broadly speaking" (*ecclesia large dicta*): the former being the body of Christ, the latter the mixed multitude of the Church visible.[1]

This does not mean that we are supposed to tolerate hypocrites; it just means that their presence does not "unchurch" us. Even after the hypocrites have infiltrated the Church, the Church remains, and remains worth defending. So discipline is important, but does not have *definitional* importance. "Calvin's ecclesiology is distinguished from that of some of his successors by his perception that discipline, for all its importance to him, belonged not to the *esse* of the Church but to its *bene esse*."[2] In the same way, "Zwingli's frequent use of the parable of the wheat and the tares underlines his acceptance of the mixed nature of the Church."[3] The "first gathered Church of sectarian Protestantism" was not formed until

---

[1] Paul Avis, *The Church*, 28.
[2] Ibid., 35.
[3] Ibid., 46.

1525.[4] But since that time, sect-theology has become pervasive in the Protestant world, and people have even come to believe that this mentality represents the Protestant Reformation. Thus, at the sign of the first heretic, they bolt and run. But this is not Protestant; it is not even Puritan. This mindset is antithetical to the Reformed view of the Church.

> In England, both William Perkins, an "establishment" puritan concerned above all for the effective cure of souls, and Thomas Cartwright, a radical puritan . . . who later conformed and wrote against the separatists, held that discipline was necessary to the well-being (*bene esse*) of the Church but not absolutely indispensible to its existence (*esse*).[5]

So of course heretics should be disciplined. But suppose they are not. The Church does not disappear fifteen minutes after the first missed heresy trial. Lampstands can be removed, but it takes more to accomplish this than is supposed by modern doctrinal perfectionists.

[4] Ibid., 52.
[5] Ibid., 46.

17
Sons of Belial

One of the great problems we have in this discussion of the covenant is that of terminology. What do we call these people within the covenant who do not understand the first thing about it? We have already considered the heretics, but there are a large number of people who are not smart enough to be heretics. What do we call them? In the New Testament usage, heretics appear to be teachers or leaders in some sense. What do we call those who do not quite fit this description?

Within the covenant, we find that the Scriptures speak frequently of fruitless members of the covenant. The idea of fruitless branches which we find in the New Testament is not something which originates there. The Scripture speaks throughout the Old Testament of "children of Belial." The word Belial carries connotations of worthlessness, without profit—or as we would say, *empty* and *hollow*.

"But these speak evil of those things which they know not: but what they know naturally, as brute beasts, in those things they corrupt themselves" (Jude 10–13). The problem that Jude was confronting was the fact that such fellows had joined themselves to faithful covenant members and were with them at the feast. Now these men were probably also false teachers and so would fall under the issues addressed in the previous chapter. But there appears to be another element here as well.

What are we to make of the phrase "sons of Belial"? In every
instance of the phrase in the Old Testament, it always refers to
members of the covenant whose lives were completely at odds
with the terms of it, and whose hollowness was exhibited in their
behavior. Pagan unbelievers from Babylon or Assyria are not
identified with this phrase. It appears to refer to blockhead covenant members. And as we consider what they were like, we see
that disobedience within the covenant can get pretty gross.

Perverts are sons of Belial—the men who abused the Levite's
concubine were called by this phrase (Judg. 19:22;20:13). Drunk-
ards are children of Belial—Hannah was afraid that Eli would
mistake her for such a worthless daughter (1 Sam. 1:16). Unconverted men are sons of Belial—the sons of Eli were worthless in
this way (1 Sam. 2:12). They did not know the Lord. Tyrants are
sons of Belial—the sons of Eli give us a number of characteristics.
They helped themselves in an autocratic way, abusing their authority (1 Sam. 2:14). Fornicators are sons of Belial—again, the
sons of Eli show us what this is like (1 Sam. 2:22). False witnesses
are sons of Belial—when Naboth was murdered, it was the work
of such men (1 Kgs. 21:10,13). Idolaters are sons of Belial—the
law warns against idolatrous enticement from such fools (Deut.
13:13). Political mutterers are sons of Belial—when Saul became
king, these were the men who held back from supporting him (1
Sam. 10:27). Pigheaded husbands are sons of Belial—Nabal is the
poster child for this scriptural category, according to both his ser-
vants and wife (1 Sam. 25:17, 25). Grabbers are sons of Belial—
when David won a victory over a raiding party, the sons of Belial
in his band did not want to share the spoil with those who
couldn't keep up the pace (1 Sam. 30:22). Rebels are sons of
Belial—political factionalism is another characteristic (2 Sam.
20:1; cf., 2 Chr.. 13:7).

David was a glorious king over Israel, and his last words addressed the necessity of disciplining the sons of Belial—and he
taught how they must be handled roughly. They cannot be taken
with the hands but must be thrust away (2 Sam. 23:1–7). David

was speaking about sons of Belial at court, but the principle applies to every congregation of God's people, under every circum-
stance. This applies to the family, to the civil order, and to the
Church. When the works of the flesh (which are manifest) erupt
in any godly assembly, the only appropriate response is firm discipline. But we never discipline because someone *might be* a son of
Belial in his heart. We discipline because his behavior has made it
plain.

The one instance of this word in the New Testament includes
all these Old Testament connotations, but has picked up an important additional meaning. In the intertestamental period, the word
Belial became synonymous with the devil, and so became associated with pure unbelief—outside the covenant. But the people of
God still have to be warned against importing this kind of infidelity into the covenant. We are to maintain distinctions and separate
ourselves from sons of Belial—those who want to have it both
ways, those who want to eat at two tables (2 Cor. 6:11–18).

One basic duty of the saints is to hate every form of unholiness. This includes unholiness within the covenant—even when
that unholiness must remain there because we cannot get at it
yet.

When we can lawfully do so, we must administer Church discipline. Of course, there are instances when this kind of covenantal
worthlessness can be reached by means of Church discipline. And
when it can be, we are to obey the Scriptures. The Scriptures say
that if you strike the fool, the simple learn wisdom (Prov. 19:25).
But even if he doesn't, he will likely lay low. This is how we see
that Church discipline is not a net designed to catch every disobedient fish. In the meantime, admonish and rebuke, and if that
doesn't work, *mark* and *avoid* such individuals. Make sure the standards you apply are scriptural standards, but if they are then
adopt the standard put so well by Joshua, "As for me and my
house, we will serve the Lord." Pursuing the peace of the
Church does not entail silence when covenant members are
defying the Word.

18

False Brothers

How do we describe members of the covenant who deny that same covenant with their words and lives? We have talked about this same question under the headings of "heretics" and "sons of Belial," but another word used in Scripture for this is *false*. But the word *false* does not refer to their covenant membership, but rather to their words and lives. It is the reality of their covenant membership that makes them false. Learning this distinction will also help us make good gospel sense out of the law/gospel dichotomy.

False brothers should be considered both as brothers and as being false. The concept of covenant-breaking helps us to make sense of this.

> And that because of false brethren unawares brought in, who came in privily to spy out our liberty which we have in Christ Jesus, that they might bring us into bondage . . . . (Gal. 2:4)

The apostle Paul came with Barnabas and met with the leaders of the church at Jerusalem. Here, in the highest circles of the church, were false brothers (not known openly as such), and they were trying to spy out the nature of the liberty of grace and seeking to bring the freed church back into bondage.

Note the correlations: *false* with *bondage*, and *Christ Jesus* with *liberty*. Or, put another way, we have the collision between law and gospel—not that the law as God gave it is false, but a certain pharisaical understanding of it certainly is. We find danger from false brothers (2 Cor. 11:26). There are many false prophets (1 Jn. 4:1). False prophets in the past are a portent of false teachers in the future (2 Pet. 2:1–2). Such false workers are usually decked out in all the right covenant garb (2 Cor. 11:13–15). They do not walk up to people and identify themselves as liars.

There are two kinds of covenant members. We need to be careful that we do not think as children. The Word of God is unified, but the reason we see it as divided is that we have to account for two kinds of people, each group seeing the Word as unified, but in different ways. But the Scriptures are not divided up into law portions in one section and grace portions in another. We do, however, have law-readers and grace-readers.

Law-readers see it all as law and stumble over the gospel, which is foolishness to them (1 Cor. 1:18). Grace-readers see it all as grace and delight in God's kindness everywhere. The law of the Lord is perfect, converting the soul (Ps. 19:7). The preamble of the Ten Commandments, "the words of this law," is a recital of God's gracious salvation of Israel from Egypt (Exod. 20:2). The converted heart looks at the Scripture and sees God's goodness, kindness and grace everywhere. The self-righteous heart looks at the Scripture and sees a list of things for self to do in order to place God in debt to that self.

This is no surprise to God. The Scriptures teach us about these two kinds of readers. One mindset desires a righteousness that is of the law. "For Moses describeth the righteousness which is of the law, That the man which doeth those things shall live by them" (Rom. 10:5). The man that "doeth" autonomously, the man who trusts in himself—such a man is going about to establish the kind of righteousness that he can take some pride in. Such a one chokes on the bread of life. Such men want to will, do, achieve, earn, merit something. But the only thing a sinner can actually earn is his own damnation, for "the wages of sin is death."

The only alternative is a righteousness that is of faith— "But the righteousness which is of faith speaketh on this wise . . . that if thou shalt confess with thy mouth the Lord Jesus, and shalt believe in thine heart that God hath raised him from the dead, thou shalt be saved" (Rom. 10:6–9). This confession was originally given in Deuteronomy concerning the law, which was not up in heaven or across the sea. Moses said that the Israelites were not to say that the law was up in heaven and too hard to get to. They were not to say that it was across the sea and impossible to achieve. It was near them, in their hearts and in their mouths. On the basis of this exhortation about the *law*, Paul says that this meant we are not to say that *Christ* is up in heaven and unattainable, or that He descended to death and cannot be brought up from the grave. On the basis of this we say that Christ is the heart and soul of the law, to everyone who believes (Rom. 10:4). The believing heart looks at the prohibition of stealing, for example, and sees Jesus Christ. The unbelieving heart looks at the gospel of Christ and sees something to earn.

Both these mindsets are found within the covenant people of God. Moses addressed both of them. To the first group, he warned them that the one who does these things shall live by them. Perfection is required. To the second group, he says that Christ is in their hearts and in their mouths. But in both instances he is speaking to circumcised Jews.

Now the reason we have two kinds of covenant members is that we have, in effect, two "covenants," corresponding in their turn to the blessings and curses of the one covenant. One "covenant" consists of those who by grace "get it." The other "covenant" is the sin-made covenant of falsehood, lies, and bondage *within the context* of surrounding grace. It is, in effect, a covenant that hardhearted people have made to break covenant.

Paul tells us this expressly. "For it is written, that Abraham had two sons, the one by a bondmaid, the other by a freewoman . . . Which things are an allegory: *for these are the two covenants*; the one from the mount Sinai, which gendereth to bondage, which is Agar" (Gal. 4:22–24). Of course the other covenant is the covenant proper—the mother of all the *free* children. In other words, Paul looked at the visible covenant people of God and saw a covenant to break covenant alongside the keepers of the covenant God had established in truth.

Repeated warnings in the New Testament show us that this development of an "anti-covenant" within the covenant is not just present in the Old Testament. As long as there are sinners in the world, some of them will pretend to embrace the gospel of grace and will get it upside down and backwards. The fact that they have to use "grace words" to disguise their legalism barely slows such unbelievers down. Paul issues a warning against this sin in a New Covenant gospel context.

> Let us therefore fear, lest, a promise being left us of entering into his rest, any of you should seem to come short of it. For unto us was the gospel preached, as well as unto them: but the Word preached did not profit them, not being mixed with faith in them that heard it. For we which have believed do enter into rest . . .(Heb. 4:1–3a)

And he does the same thing again in 1 Corinthians. The Corinthians were beginning to put on airs over against the Jews. "We are baptized. We have the Lord's Supper." "Oh, yeah?" Paul replies. "*So did they.*"

> Moreover, brethren, I would not that ye should be ignorant, how that all our fathers were under the cloud, and all passed through the sea; And were all baptized unto Moses in the cloud and in the sea; And did all eat the same spiritual meat; And did all drink the same spiritual drink: for they drank of that spiritual Rock that followed them: and that Rock was Christ. But with many of them God was not well pleased: for they were overthrown in the wilderness. *Now these things were our examples,*

to the intent we should not lust after evil things, as they also
lusted. (1 Cor. 10:1–6)

In other words, Paul warns a New Testament church about the
parallels between their situation and the Jews in the wilderness,
and he does so at just the place where modern Christians tend to
draw contrasts.

And so what is the application? *Stop trying to pick up grace.* You
have no hands. Grace picks you up, out of the miry clay, and sets
your feet on the rock. A true heart knows this.

The presence of false brothers does not unsettle the faith of
those who are true. How could it? This is all explained to us in
the Scriptures. Calvin's comment is apropos:

> Here, then, a twofold class of sons presents itself to us, in the
> Church; for since the whole body of the people is gathered to-
> gether into the fold of God, by one and the same voice, all
> without exception, are, in this respect, accounted children; the
> name of the Church is applicable to them all: but in the inner-
> most sanctuary of God, none others are reckoned the sons of
> God, that they in whom the promise is ratified by faith. And al-
> though this difference flows from the fountain of gratuitous
> election, whence also faith itself springs; yet, since the counsel
> of God is in itself hidden from us, we therefore distinguish the
> true from the spurious children, by the respective marks of
> faith and of unbelief.[†]

[†] John Calvin, *Calvin's Commentaries* (Grand Rapids: Baker, 1979), 1:449.

19

Blessings and Curses

We must learn how to speak with scriptural language, rather than with the misleading language that comes from our feeble efforts at reasoning. For example, when we learn that the covenant contains both blessings and curses, our tendency is to say that it must be "the covenant of blessings and curses." But Paul speaks of the cup of blessing, not the cup "of blessing and cursing." We must not just learn the fact of covenant curses, but also the place and purpose of them, and the need for proper interpretation.

> Who is he that saith, and it cometh to pass, when the Lord commandeth it not? Out of the mouth of the most High proceedeth not evil and good? Wherefore doth a living man complain, a man for the punishment of his sins? Let us search and try our ways, and turn again to the LORD. Let us lift up our heart with our hands unto God in the heavens. (Lam. 3:37–41)

We see here that God ordains all things. No one can speak in such a way as to make events go contrary to the Lord's commands. Out of the Lord's mouth we see His decrees concerning both evil and good. So why should any mortal complain when he receives punishment for his sins? Rather than assuming that the decrees of heaven are inscrutable, such a man is commanded to search out and test his own ways so that he might repent rightly. The end result is the right worship of God, a heart lifted up before God with both hands.

As we consider covenantal cause and effect, we have to guard ourselves against two errors. The first is the error of presumption, where someone takes it upon himself to declare what was in the mind of God for every little thing. In other words, "Murphy got a flat tire today because three days ago he was cross with his wife." The opposite error is one that appears at first glance to be a very humble approach. "We know that God has ordained all things, but we can never draw any conclusions about why unless we are claiming that we have the gift of prophecy."

The former error overspecifies and the latter underspecifies. And while the former error can be a nuisance, in our day it has not stumbled nearly as many people as the latter error has. Too many Christians imitate the Scottish philosopher David Hume who decided that because he could not "see" causation, it wasn't there. They cannot see the direct connection between the providence of God and the particular chastisement that occurred to them. When it comes to covenantal cause and effect, they seek to remain agnostic. But this means they cannot interpret how their life is going at all.

Scripture teaches us that God expects us to understand the world around us. This is just another way of saying that we are called to interpret the "good" things and the "bad" things that happen to us in terms of covenantal blessings and chastisements, and we are to modify our behavior accordingly. We are not to do this woodenly. This is what Job's friends did, and they sinned against Job (Job 42:7). This is what the disciples did when they asked one time about the cause of a man's blindness (Jn. 9:2). We are called to make such assessments in all wisdom.

We need covenant feedback. Without nerve endings and the pain and pleasure they bring, we would all quickly destroy ourselves. In order to live prudently with our bodies, we need feedback from the environment which tells us what is harmful and what is not. In the same way, we need covenant feedback. "Do so more and more" comes in the form of covenant blessings. "Knock that off" comes in the form of covenant chastisement and admonition.

The Bible is clear at this point. "Be not deceived; God is not mocked: for whatsoever a man soweth, that shall he also reap. For he that soweth to his flesh shall of the flesh reap corruption; but he that soweth to the Spirit shall of the Spirit reap life ever-lasting. And let us not be weary in well doing: for in due season we shall reap, if we faint not" (Gal. 6:7–9).

When we bow our heads to say grace, how do we know to *thank* God for the food? Is this a blessing to my family or not? Am I a prophet? How do I know that God is not fattening us all up for the day of slaughter? Is this a real blessing? How can I know? The answer is that we know these things by faith. God explains to us how the world generally runs, and we submit to Him in that gov-ernance of the world, and so we thank Him for good things and search our hearts and motives when bad things happen. We do this knowing that covenant-breakers can receive good things for a time and that covenant-keepers may go through rough waters.

We have to take care that we do not make any of these evalua-tions on the basis of short term thinking—in the passage from Galatians considered a moment ago, we saw that in "due season" we shall reap. The same thing is true in Hebrews 12:11. *Afterward* godly submission to discipline yields the peaceable fruit of righ-teousness.

We also have to reject simplistic thinking and not do what Job's friends did. Those who taunted Jesus on the cross were three days off in their calculations. The short term results looked grim, but Jesus was in the process of conquering the world. We need to wait for the rest of the story. As far as the simple are concerned, vindications do not come in a timely way. And another kind of simplistic thinking maintains that vindications in this world never come. But both fall short of biblical wisdom.

Humility brings wisdom—and wisdom brings further humil-ity. Rebuke a wise man and he loves you (Prov. 9:8). This de-meanor means that wisdom is sensitive to the messages embedded in the world.

And of course thanksgiving sanctifies—everything that God
created is good, and it may all be received with thanksgiving
(1 Tim. 4:4–5). The one who *cannot* do this is actually being chas-
tised. We are to give thanks for all things, so this includes our tri-
als (Eph. 5:20). The blessings and curses that come to us are
therefore not a puzzle to be solved, but rather a gift to be received in all humility and thanksgiving.

We emphasize the curses of the covenant as a reality to be
noted, and not a threat to hang over ourselves every minute. But
faithfulness to the Word requires that we understand that every
covenant with men has attendant blessings and curses. Greg
Bahnsen notes:

> So, those who are in the Church, but not elect, are nevertheless
> within the Covenant of grace, *but under its curse.* The Covenant of
> Grace curses people who have the privilege of being among God's
> people on earth distinguished from the world and yet don't live up
> to what He teaches. That's why the Church sometimes has to in-
> tervene, lest the Church profane God's covenant and its seals. My
> only point is that you couldn't write that unless you believed that
> the non-elect, who were being disciplined, are in the covenant.[1]

To some, this might seem covenantally morbid but only until
we realize how many theological problems the *category* of covenant curses solves. Bahnsen again:

> To be covenantally united with God, although intended by God to
> bring favor and blessing to His chosen people, carries *as well* the
> threat of judgment and curse. God's covenants involve *blessing and
> cursing*, depending upon whether one is a covenant-keeper or a
> covenant-breaker.[2]

In this there is food for the soul—we are enabled to take all scriptural warnings to heart. At the same time, there is rest for the
theological mind—and the heart of faith.

[1] Qtd. in Booth, 52. Emphasis mine.
[2] Qtd. in ibid., 53.

Part IV

Justification and Good Works

20

Resurrected Law

In the resurrection of Jesus Christ, all things are made new. Unfortunately, too many of us take this as the spiritual equivalent of Christians being able to have a spring in their step. But the meaning that the Scriptures assign to this is nothing less than inevitability of cosmic renovation. And this includes all things, the law of God being no exception.

When Jesus died, the law died. And when He rose again, so did the law. "Blotting out the handwriting of ordinances that was against us, which was contrary to us, and took it out of the way, nailing it to his cross" (Col. 2:13–17).

When the Bible talks about the cross of Jesus Christ, it of course talks about *our* inclusion in that death. We are sinners, and in the death of Jesus our old man is put to death. Paul says that he had been crucified with Christ (Gal. 2:20), and as a consequence, he also shared in the life of Christ's resurrection. But there is also plain teaching that more than just elect sinners died "with and in" Christ. The Bible teaches that the law also was crucified. What are we to make of this?

In the text above from Colossians, the "handwriting of ordinances that was against us," that was "contrary to us," was taken out of the way and nailed to the cross of Christ—and there perished. On the basis of this, we are then commanded to let no one judge us in terms of the shadowy requirements of the law (vv. 16–17). All the law, including what we are accustomed to call "moral law," is included here.

In a similar passage from Ephesians, Paul says that when God was making one new man (Christian) out of two (Jew and Gentile), He did this by crucifying a portion of His holy law. The enmity between Jew and Gentile is defined as the "law of commandments contained in ordinances" (v. 15). A subset of the law is meant here. And God took care of that enmity by crucifying it in the body of Christ.

We hear such things and we tend to panic. If the law is dead, then how shall we govern our lives? At this point, many Christians divide into two different camps represented by the words *continuity* and *discontinuity*.

Many of those who argue for continuity say that we still have the law of God in the Old Testament continuing over into the New in just the same kind of way. Many of those who argue for discontinuity say that the old law is dead, and good riddance; we are now directed by the "Spirit within" or by express teaching in the "New Testament only."

So which is it? The answer is both—the law has complete continuity in the same way that the body of Christ had continuity with His resurrection body. It was the same body that rose from the dead (Jn. 20:27). The law has discontinuity in the sense that the resurrection changes the meaning and nature of everything. "And that which thou sowest, thou sowest not that body that shall be" (1 Cor. 15:37). In the death of Jesus, the law of God died. In the resurrection of Jesus, the law of God rose from the dead. In that death and resurrection, the law remained what it was and was also transformed in a glorious way.

We are God's people by covenant, and the same principles apply here as well. The new covenant is not like the covenant God made with our fathers (Jer. 31:31). In part the covenant is new because the law governing the covenant is new. But by *new*, we do not mean "freshly invented" but rather "back from the dead." There cannot be a change in the priesthood without a corresponding change in the law. But the priesthood has been bestowed on

Christ on the basis of His power of an indestructible life. The change of the law in Him shares in this resurrection life. As Paul says, "Ye are our epistle written in our hearts, known and read of all men: Forasmuch as ye are manifestly declared to be the epistle of Christ ministered by us, written not with ink, but with the Spirit of the living God; not in tables of stone, but in fleshy tables of the heart" (2 Cor. 3:2–3). Risen from the dead, the law is now written on human hearts.

There are a number of practical applications from this. In all things obedience is life, and every form of pseudo-obedience is death.

First, negatively, we need to take care that we obey nothing *external*, nothing that has not been internalized by means of death and resurrection. "For they being ignorant of God's righteousness, and going about to establish their own righteousness, have not submitted themselves unto the righteousness of God. For Christ is the end of the law for righteousness to every one that believeth" (Rom. 10:3–4). Believeth what? In the death, burial and resurrection of Jesus Christ. Every form of external obedience is an attempt to "go about" to establish a self-centered righteousness. This is because if the "obedience" is external to an uncrucified heart, then that uncrucified heart will attempt to take sole credit for whatever occurs. This is what the flesh does, and has to do.

Second, we must recognize that resurrected law is law that lives and breathes, and is law that liberates in *the same way life does*. "For the law of the Spirit of life in Christ Jesus hath made me free from the law of sin and death. For what the law could not do . . ." (Rom. 8:1–4). Living wisdom is never inanimate. Scripture does not recognize a difference between law and love, or between obedience and wisdom. All of it lives. A living man is free to walk around. A man who has been brought to life spiritually is now capable of walking away from sin and death.

Third, we should recognize that this passage from death to life *does* alter the standards of the law, externally understood, but not by *lowering* them. "For I say unto you, That except your righteousness shall exceed the righteousness of the scribes and Pharisees, ye shall in no case enter into the kingdom of heaven" (Mt. 5:20). But at the same time, the law of the Spirit is not "rigorist," any more than you and I are now "rigorously" alive.

And fourth, we need to notice how obedience is rendered. "Neither yield ye your members as instruments of unrighteousness unto sin: but yield yourselves unto God, *as those that are alive from the dead*, and your members as instruments of righteousness unto God. For sin shall not have dominion over you: for ye are not under the law, but under grace. What then? shall we sin, because we are not under the law, but under grace? God forbid" (Rom. 6:13–15). We who are resurrected from the dead in Christ, along with our fellow resurrectee, the law, should take care that we talk sense.

It is important for us to understand the nature of new covenant law as resurrected law because to fail to do so is to drift back into troublesome law/gospel distinctions. And of course, faith is never legalistic because faith operates in the realm of new life. And works by themselves are always dead.

This is why faith always sees the grace of God everywhere, even in the law. As John Frame put it,

> But it should be evident that "legalist" preaching as described above is not true preaching of law. For as I indicated earlier, law itself in Scripture comes to us wrapped in grace.[†]

The law is holy, righteous, and good. And now that it has risen together with Jesus Christ, as have all true believers, it need no longer terrify us.

[†] John Frame, "Law and Gospel," (<http://www.chalcedon.edu/articles/0201/020104frame.shtml>).

We honor and love the Scriptures, and so we seek to live the way the Word requires. One of the things required by that Word is the building of Christ's Church over the course of generations. And one of the great problems that confronts us as we seek to build, honor, and love this institutional Church, and as we seek to be faithful to work of the Holy Spirit in the historical Church, is that we tend to forget the glory that is in our midst, and we abandon our authority in order to teach like the scribes. Because we have forgotten the permanent things, newness of life becomes dull to us. The answer to this problem is always the same—the clarion call of the gospel, death and life, agony and triumph.

This is what our baptism means. "Therefore we are buried with him by baptism into death: that like as Christ was raised up from the dead by the glory of the Father, even so we also should walk *in newness of life*" (Romans 6:4). In this passage, the apostle Paul shows the daily relevance of the great gospel realities. Christ did not die so that we might live. He died so that we might die, and He lives so that we might live. Our life is not tied to His death—our life is tied to His life. But we cannot be tied to His life unless we have also been united with Him in His death.

Shall we continue in sin because of His grace (v. 1)? Of course not. We cannot continue in that state of sin because we have died to it (v. 2). This is the meaning of our baptisms, and the import of them—baptism is the funeral of sin (v. 3). But the good news is that our union with Christ does not end at the baptism of death—we are raised with Him to newness of life (v. 4). This is the meaning of Easter. God's pattern is to unite us with death and then with resurrection (v. 5). Our union with His death was so that the body of our sin might be demolished (v. 6). What liberates from sin? Death (v. 7). And the necessary connection between death and resurrection is emphasized again (v. 8). Death is definitive (v. 9). You die once, you are baptized *once*. You live continually before God (v. 10). Our duty therefore is to consider this to be so (v. 11). Believe it. And this has an immediate and drastic effect on what you do with your body (vv. 12–13). Our annual and weekly commemoration of the resurrection declare the advent of the reign of grace, in which we live (v. 14).

The Lord Jesus took on flesh, lived a perfect sinless life, suffered on the cross under Pontius Pilate, was buried in the tomb of another man, rose from the dead on the third day in accordance with the Scriptures, appeared to the women, then to His other disciples, and ascended into heaven with great majesty, was enthroned at the right hand of God the Father, and since that time has exercised universal dominion over all nations. Through the gospel of grace, through faith alone, we are invited to participate in all of this. But how do we "get on?" The place where we join Him is in His death—not His birth, not His glorification, not His resurrection. We are *baptized* into His death. That baptism is our introduction to union with Him.

God has a signature, and has identifiable handwriting. In this fallen world, He testifies to His goodness in the universal pattern of death and resurrection. Every day you get sleepy, lie down, and rise up. Every autumn the trees of the forest and grass in the field wither and every spring they come back in glory.

The apostle says that these things are so—but then he hastens to add that believers are called to act as though it is so. Reckon it to be so. This means, by inference, that it is possible (but not right) for baptized believers to act in their lives as though the gospel were not true. How many conservative husbands are outraged if some liberal preacher says that Jesus did not rise from the dead, when their daily treatment of their wives makes the same statement? At least the liberal only states his heresy occasionally.

The objective meaning of the gospel is unchanged by our hypocrisies. But *we* are not unchanged by our hypocrisies. The

Lord has risen—we must act as though it is so. Reckon yourselves to be dead to sin but alive to God in Christ Jesus.

As we walk in newness of life, what are the areas where this newness is most visible? In all such areas, for the believer walking in the light, glory is suffused throughout the ordinary. That glory has weight, and it brings home a glad reality. This includes the glory of newness in worship—man was created to worship God. We are becoming fully human as we worship. It includes the glory of newness in marriage and family— there are only two options in the home: death or life. Then there is the glory of newness in work—we discover that forgiven hands are the hands of Christ. The hands of Christ *work* in full accordance with resurrected law. We also see the glory of newness in creational celebration—we learn that the whole world declares the glory of God. And so should we.

This glory of newness is gladness and simplicity of heart— when we understand the meaning of the resurrection of Jesus Christ, we come to understand grace, law, sabbath, rest, peace, life, and joy inexpressible.

21

The Greatness of Justification by Faith

We have already considered what the Bible teaches about justification and the justified individual, considered *as* an individual. In this limited sense, the historic Protestant position on justification is correct, and the Roman Catholic understanding of individual justification as a process involving an infusion of righteousness is wrong. But having said this, we have to acknowledge that we have not exhausted the biblical teaching on justification.

The logical error of bifurcation is frequently tangled up in this. It makes sense, for example, to say that the car is either blue or it is not blue. In saying this, we exhaust the options. These are the only two. But if we say that the car is either blue or red, a number of other colors that it could be come immediately to mind. It is the same with justification.

It is simplistic to assume that the Bible speaks of justification in only one way. The fact that justification in one sense is forensic in nature (i.e., one is "declared righteous in Christ") is not diminished by the assertion that in another sense one is justified by works. "You see then that a man is justified by works, and not by faith only. Likewise, was not Rahab the harlot also justified by works when she received the messengers and sent them out another way? For as the body without the spirit is dead, so faith without works is dead also" (Jas. 2:24-26). This second sense of justification is a demonstration of the reality, or fact, of the first sense of forensic justification.[1]

We maintain that we are not justified by our good works, but that we are justified to good works (Eph. 2:10). In saying this, we have to refer back to an earlier chapter on systematics as an exercise in interpretation, and not replacement. We also have to say, using biblical language, that we are justified by good works.

These good works, done in obedience to God's commandments, are the fruits and evidences of a true and lively faith: and by them believers manifest their thankfulness, strengthen their assurance, edify their brethren, adorn the profession of the gospel, stop the mouths of the adversaries, and glorify God, whose workmanship they are, created in Christ Jesus thereunto, that, having their fruit unto holiness, they may have the end, eternal life. (16:2)

These good works are not in themselves the ground of salvation, but they are the ground of assurance of salvation. They are the fruit of the tree, not the cause of the tree. They are the evidence that the tree is alive and growing. They are fruit and evidence of a true and lively faith. Good works are instruments through which believers show how thankful they are. This also has the result of fortifying assurance of salvation. Good works are a blessing and edification to other believers, and unbelievers see in the good works an adornment to the gospel itself. Those nonbelievers still disposed to kick against the faith are shut down by our good works. All our works together, in all their relations and effects, have the end result of glorifying God. This is because our works are His works, and when we do them, He is glorified for doing them. The end of the tale is eternal life.

[1] Booth, 35.

Their ability to do good works is not at all of themselves, but wholly from the Spirit of Christ. And that they may be enabled thereunto, beside the graces they have already received, there is required an actual influence of the same Holy Spirit, to work in them to will, and to do, of His good pleasure: yet are they not hereupon to grow negligent, as if they were not bound to perform any duty unless upon a special motion of the Spirit; but they ought to be diligent in stirring up the grace of God that is in them. (16:3)

We are called to work out only what God has worked in. We are dependent upon Him in two senses. First, we depend upon the initial grace that He has given us, but we are also dependent upon the present prompting of the Spirit to particular good deeds—what we might call a "burden." This does not mean we may sit around the house waiting for a burden from the Lord, but rather that we should seek to stir up the grace of God so that we recover any burdens we may have lost.

Consequently, in the historic Protestant view, good works are inseparable from biblical salvation. They are not a condiment to flavor a "raw" justification, but rather are definitionally related to justification. Justification and sanctification are not like salt and pepper, or ham and eggs—two things that go well together. They are definitionally interrelated, like the terms *husband* and *wife*. If there is no wife, then by definition there is no husband. If there is no husband, then by definition there is no wife. Apart from sanctification, justification does not exist. Apart from justification, sanctification does not exist. We distinguish the two readily, but we cannot separate them. We should be able to tell at a glance who is the husband and who is the wife—but we cannot remove one without removing the other.

Because this is the case, James can speak of justification by works. He is not speaking of rabbinical works-righteousness, or Pelagian self-salvation, or of medieval merit theology. Rather, he compares it to the relationship of body and spirit—a living, organic entity. We distinguish body and spirit, but we cannot remove one without removing the other. Protestant creedal formulations have found it (rightly) necessary to remind people that husbands aren't wives. But we now find it necessary to remind people that husbands have wives.

Complicating the matter (a little) further, we find that the Scriptures also frequently refer to a *corporate* justification of God's people that is highly visible. This corporate justification begins with the justification of Jesus, our Head, which cannot be thought of as justification in the tradition of crisis conversions. "As Richard Gaffin has argued, the resurrection of Jesus is the ground of our justification (Rom. 4:25) because it is first of all the vindication (justification) of Jesus (1 Tim. 3:16)."[2]

In his key essay on this subject, Leithart demonstrates that in Scripture judges do not just declare sentences, but they also execute them. He also shows that in Genesis 15, the meaning of "reckoned righteous" has to take this covenantal aspect and understanding into account. In a number of places in the Psalms and prophets, the biblical writers describe justification as just such a public vindication. And last, Leithart shows that these Old Testament categories *are very much in Paul's mind* as he teaches on "the righteousness of God" that is revealed in the gospel. None of this means that the traditional Protestant understanding of the righteousness of Christ imputed to individuals is wrong or misplaced. It simply means that individual justification is operating in a far grander context than perhaps some Protestants have thought.

> Abram was under the curse of death, and his request that Yahweh keep His promises included a request to be delivered from this "sentence." Hence, the Reformation doctrine of justification has Pauline precedent. Yet, second, it is also clear that

---

[2] Peter Leithart, "'Judge Me, O God': Biblical Perspectives on Justification" (<http://www.hornes.org/theologia/content/peter_leithart/judge_me_o_god_biblical_perspectives_on_justification.htm>).

forgiveness and being reckoned righteous do not exhaust what Paul means by "justification."[3]

Our corporate justification as the Church was Pentecostal. God publicly vindicated us, owned us as His people, and established us in the world as His own righteous people. This means that the Church *as the Church* is justified, just as the Church is elect, and redeemed, and so forth. But this also means that nonelect covenant members, while truly attached to the body, are nevertheless an incongruity—spots and blemishes that will be removed as the Bride is made radiant. But in the meantime, until they are removed, we have to learn to deal with nonelect members of the Elect One, and unjustified members of the Justified Body.

> Only faithful covenant members (i.e., those full of faith in the Savior), receive the covenant blessings, including the blessing of imputed righteousness.[4]

This is fundamental to the central point of this book. Election is one thing and covenant membership is another. And this distinction is no theological innovation.

> Lillback concludes that "Calvin did not let the pressures of his theological system cause him to identify the covenant and election. This would have seemingly closed the door on many intricate questions. Yet, Calvin believed the Scriptures required the distinction between the covenant and secret election."[5]

As the people of God, we exhibit to the world what it means to be right with God, to be living under the "righteousness of God." Individuals are put right with God as individuals,

---

[3] Ibid.
[4] Booth, 32.
[5] Ibid., 52.

families as families, churches as churches, and the Church as the Church. In order to be right with God, two fundamental attitudes are necessary, corresponding to the two central scriptural gospel commands—*repent* and *believe*. The first attitude is that of contrition and repentance, and of course this means honest self-examination. It does *not* mean perpetual morbidity. The second is faith in *all* of God's promises. The problem with pietistic Christians is that they get stuck in the first mode, and never move on to the second. We can tell if we are stuck in this way if we can see potential disparities between scriptural prayers and our prayers.

For example, consider this psalm. "Judge me, O Lord my God, according to thy righteousness; and let them not rejoice over me" (Ps. 35:24). Shall not the judge of the whole earth do right? God is our judge. We know we have gotten stuck in repentance mode when we hear this as meaning simply and solely that He is the one who will determine whether or not to destroy us with a divine lightning bolt. In the Scriptures, particularly in the Psalms, *God as Judge* is indistinguishable from *God as Deliverer*. When God judges His people, He is *saving* His people, *vindicating* them.

This is the cry of scriptural faith. The one who prays in this way knows himself (by faith) to be completely identified with God and the cause of His covenant people. This is believed in the bones. But of course we must maintain balance. This scriptural faith is not the same thing as a smug self-righteousness about the self-evident purity of whatever side *you* happen to be on. No, the "repentance element" of God's judgment is here as well. God is clearly seen as a hypothetical or potential adversary. We should never neglect our duty of repentance, but we must always go on to the weightier matters of salvation. We go on to *faith*.

So of course we know that in any controversy between us and the Lord, we would be condemned. "And enter not into judgment with thy servant: for in thy sight shall no man living be justified" (Ps. 143:2). And we know that if we were condemned, it would be for our individual failings. "If thou, Lord, shouldest mark iniquities, O Lord, who shall stand?" (Ps. 130:3). We do not deny the need for confession and repentance. But this is what we do at the entrance. We wipe our feet at the door. But there are other things to do *inside* God's great household.

Too many devout Christians have assumed that to be mindful of the judgment of God is to live in a state of perpetual terror and personal misgiving. As we have seen, the Scripture teaches this lesson after a fashion—for the *first* chapter of the covenant journey. But what else does God tell us about the time when He rises to judge?

The Bible teaches that judgment is salvation. "For the Lord is our judge, the Lord is our lawgiver, the Lord is our king; *he will save us*" (Is. 33:22). The primary meaning of the word *judge* should be taken from the book of *Judges*. God raises up saviors—deliverers. And in this sense, He is our ultimate Judge, and this means that He *saves*.

We also find that judgment saves the downtrodden. "And he shall judge the world in righteousness, he shall minister judgment to the people in uprightness. The Lord also will be a refuge for the oppressed, a refuge in times of trouble" (Ps. 9:8–9). In the Old Testament, even the Gentiles rejoice at the prospect of judgment. "O let the nations be glad and sing for joy: for thou shalt judge the people righteously, and govern the nations upon earth. Selah" (Ps. 67:4). There is of course always terror for the wicked, but God judges in order to put things right. Nature longs for the judgment of God. "Let the field be joyful, and all that is therein: then shall all the trees of the wood rejoice before the Lord: for he cometh, for he cometh to judge the earth: he shall judge the world with righteousness, and the people with his truth" (Ps. 96:12–13). The earth longs for judgment.

In His judgment, God rises up against the proud. "Lift up thyself, thou judge of the earth: render a reward to the proud" (Ps. 94:2). And it is not pride for *us* to pray in this way.

We are asking God to intervene and judge, and this prayer assumes that He will decide in our favor.

This is seen in a number of places. "Hear the right, O Lord, attend unto my cry, give ear unto my prayer, that goeth not out of feigned lips" (Ps. 17:1). This is astounding. A *sinner* can tell God that he is not lying and that God should therefore *listen*. "Judge me, O Lord; for I have walked in mine integrity: I have trusted also in the Lord; therefore I shall not slide" (Ps. 26:1). Why do we not pray this way? The answer is that we are stuck in repentance, with little faith.

Not only may we ask God to hear our case, we may ask Him to plead it. "Judge me, O God, and plead my cause against an ungodly nation: O deliver me from the deceitful and unjust man" (Ps. 43:1). When God takes up my cause, He is vindicating, saving, and in this certain specified sense, *justifying* me. This is a prayer that asks God to fight for my cause. "Plead my cause, O LORD, with them that strive with me: fight against them that fight against me" (Ps. 35:1). The same is true when God enters into battle on my behalf.

When we were first converted, God "judged" us in Jesus Christ. We were justified (in the proper theological sense) at that time. But since that time, we should all have learned to look to God, seeking His ongoing deliverances, historical judgments, and justifying vindications.

As the justified people of God, it is therefore our responsibility to begin to see ourselves as righteous. To be justified is to be declared righteous, and of course we are justified through faith in believing God's declarations. Far too many advocates of "worm theology" get stuck in total depravity. In other words, believe it or not, in the name of *sola fide* they wind up *not believing* what God declares to be the case. But there is a difference between the imputed righteousness of Christ and self-righteousness.

Scripture says, "The fool hath said in his heart. There is no God. They are corrupt, they have done abominable works, there is none that doeth good" (Ps. 14:1–7). The fool says there is no God (v. 1). He is corrupt and is referred to by Paul in Romans 3. No one does good. The Lord investigates from heaven to see if any understand (v. 2). They have all gone aside (v. 3). These workers of iniquity eat up God's people like they were bread (v. 4). God's people? Where did they come from, if there is *none* righteous? The answer is *grace*, and the *answer* is grace. God is in the generation of the *righteous* (v. 5). The Lord is the refuge for the poor, and evildoers have shamed them (v. 6). When salvation comes out of Zion and the captivity is ended, then Jacob shall rejoice and Israel shall be glad (v. 7).

Righteousness is therefore a judicial category. We have an unhappy tendency to use the lens of ultimate things to look at life around us. But as we have said, the ultimate things are the secret things (Deut. 29:29). So the problem is that we cannot see through the lens of ultimate things (election, for example), which is why we have a great deal of trouble making sense of what is occurring in the world around us. And so our unhappy tendency is to speak of the *saved* and the *unsaved*. But the biblical language is to speak of the *righteous* and the *wicked*. The former assumes the perspective of the eschaton while the latter assumes the perspective of the covenant, here and now.

But further, righteousness is an inescapable category. Every civic order has this division. In any society, to speak against the "justified" is to speak against what that culture considers the righteous. The only thing that varies from culture to culture is the standard of justification or righteousness—not the fact of it. Following Steve Schlissel's argument, in any society, only the righteous have the right to be offended. Taking offense is a prerogative of the righteous. The wicked, as defined *judicially* by that culture, never have the right to be offended. In our culture, victims are the new righteous, while anyone who belongs to the righteous of Jehovah is characterized *judicially* as wicked—outside the pale.

Justification does not mean perfection according to the standard. This is why you hear comments like "Well, I don't agree with everything he says or does, *but* . . . ." That *but* is the introduction to the subsequent justification. It is an introduction to what the speaker considers to be a righteous or justified *category* of people.

So unlike Abraham, we have not believed God concerning our status. This is great faithlessness on our part, but it does not affect the judicial category. We are faithless, but nevertheless we remain *the faithful*. We have been unrighteous, but nonetheless we are the righteous. Like Lot in Sodom, we are hated because of our judicial connection to Jehovah, but also like Lot in Sodom, we do not live up to God's full standard. The fact that we do not understand this is readily seen in the fact that we read Genesis and the account of Lot's life, and we would never dream of describing him as Peter does—as *righteous*. But ironically, it is when we believe God's pronouncement, despite the empirical evidence, that we first supply the empirical evidence.

This is because God will bless the righteous and encompass him around with a shield (Ps. 5:12). God intervenes to make the distinction (Ps. 7:11). God tests the one and hates the other (Ps. 11:5). And all the lies spoken about us will be revealed for what they are (Ps. 31:18). We are the righteous of the Lord. Consequently, we have certain key responsibilities within the confines of the covenant.

The first is to understand this covenant. We are objective members of an objective covenant, and this means that we have objective loyalties. One of the central loyalties is to accept and believe the terminology of the covenant. Acceptance of alien "naming" is a form of unfaithfulness to the covenant. The ungodly want to successfully name you as being wicked. Do not run ahead of them and do it for them.

The second is to discover the laws of this covenant and live by them. We do not do this to earn our righteousness; rather, we have been made members of Christ by His grace. Therefore, because we *are* the righteous we are to *live* righteously.

And third, in determining this, go where the covenant does and not where your personal likes and dislikes feel like it ought to have gone. Learn the meaning of grace, which cannot be found in a dictionary. This meaning of grace is its aroma. Having learned this, only then is it safe to learn the practical incarnational forms of grace—sacramental thanksgiving, true sabbath-keeping, psalming from the heart, and the rest of a forgiven, *righteous* life. Practical Christianity without grace is legalism. Grace without practice is gnosticism.

22

Covenant Succession

We cannot talk about covenant theology without talking about our children because our children are the heirs of the covenant. In a very real way, this debate is a debate over the theology of children. This is important because in the American church our theology of children is overwhelming baptistic, even in paedo-baptist communions. Some have joked that baby dedications in Baptist churches are actually dry baptisms. I would want to argue that it is closer to the truth, given the view of children held by many American paedo-baptists, that our infant baptisms are really wet dedications.

For example, one great Southern Presbyterian theologian—Thornwell—said that the Church was to treat her children "precisely as she treats all other impenitent and unbelieving men—she is to exercise the power of the keys, and shut them out from the communion of the saints."[1] Often a great hue and cry is lifted up against presumptive regeneration, but it is not often noticed what happens in the other direction, which is presumptive unregeneration. Dabney and Thornwell and Palmer all thought this way.

> [The] Church recognizes the majority of its minor citizens when they show that spiritual qualification—a new heart. In

[1] Schenck, *Children in the Covenant*, 94.

the meantime they were regarded as "unregenerate baptized children."[2]

This position was a doctrinal innovation and was part of the legacy of the Half-Way Covenant, followed by the impact of the Great Awakening.

> The first settlers became concerned that their grandchildren could not be baptized, since the parents of these children found themselves unable to give an account of their own regeneration which would meet the rigid requirements of the Puritans. The Half-Way Covenant was the method devised to remedy this difficulty. It permitted parents who acknowledged the claims of God in their lives and promised submission to the Church's discipline—though not professing conversion—to have their children baptized.[3]

Contrary to the assumptions of many, the Half-Way Covenant was not the result of covenantal lethargy, but just the reverse—covenantal rigorism. Everyone had to be "born again" in a highly visible, demonstrable way, but there were a number among the settlers who were not regenerate, along with a number of others who *were* regenerate but who were unable or unwilling to gin up a credible testimony. But these people believed in Christ, they held to the truth of the Christian religion, and they wanted their children baptized. They lacked a revivalistic *tremens*, but they wanted their children baptized. The Half-Way Covenant allowed for this, but maintained a high fence around the Table of the Lord. This was zeal run amok, not lethargy. Unfortunately, it was a zeal without knowledge.

A century later, the Great Awakening reinforced this doctrinal assumption in the American mentality. As a result of the Great

---

[2] Ibid., 87.
[3] Ibid., 54.

Awakening, a new assumption spread throughout Presbyterian churches.

> The presumption of regeneration in the case of children of the covenant, *based upon the covenant promises*, was largely displaced, by the Church's practice of recognizing as Christians only those who gave "credible evidence," satisfactory to themselves, of regeneration.[4]

The shift was marked. We stopped believing God's Word, and started believing converts. Before we would take any sacramental action, we had to hear from *man*. Having heard God's promises was insufficient.

Believing God's promises is faith. God gives multitudes of promises to us concerning our children. Believing them is faith. I have written on this elsewhere.[5] But for some reason, believing God's promises and living faithfully on the basis of them is routinely thought by contemporary Protestants to be a form of works. For example, Alan Strange takes it this way.

> This threat becomes a reality when the certainty of the promises of God are made dependent upon the contingency of human faithfulness. This misconceiving of covenant theology argues, for example, that when the spiritual head of a covenant home is faithful to God and his Word, the faithfulness of his wife and children is—in *ex opere operato* fashion—inevitable. This would mean in some fashion that it is the faithfulness of a man as husband and father that secures the eternal well-being of his family.[6]

---

[4] Ibid., 71. Emphasis mine.

[5] Douglas Wilson, *Standing on the Promises* (Moscow, Idaho: Canon Press, 1997), 21–31.

[6] Alan Strange, "Sacraments, The Spirit, and Human Inability," *Mid-America Journal of Theology* 12 (2001): 240.

There are several qualifications that have to be made at this point. I have argued that promises are apprehended by *faith*, not faithfulness or fidelity, but, of course, faith in the biblical sense is inseparable from faithfulness. Faith, by definition, is not faithless, but rather faithful. Faith is invisible to the human eye, but faith's constant companion—*faithfulness*—is not invisible. Nevertheless, it is *faith* that receives the promises, overthrows kingdoms, and stops the mouths of lions. If we adopt the shorthand of James, we could say that faithfulness (works) does these things also, but we would be using his shorthand.

Now if faith can stop the mouth of lions, does that make stopping lions' mouths by faith an *ex opere operato* action? In the same way, faith in the promises of God concerning our children is the instrument that God uses to accomplish the fulfillment of His promises. We do not manipulate God by our autonomous works into anything. We cannot raise faithful children if we bring them up in a home characterized by frantic works-righteousness.

This is a crucial point that Strange misses.

> But we must at every point recognize that it is not because of our merit in any sense (including our faithfulness) that God blesses us and it is only by the grace of God that the power of the Holy Spirit works that blessing in our lives. The divine grace that is bestowed to wives and children is not automatic and is certainly not because of husbandly fidelity. Wilson may well agree with this, yet his position, implying that human fidelity produces inevitable head-for-head results, misses the covenantal mark and heads in a biologistic *ex opere operato* direction.[7]

We must constantly remember that we have a natural and very dangerous tendency to immediately assume that keeping the covenant is accomplished by some means other than faith working its way out in love. But when we have faith that works its way out in love, which is the only thing that genuine faith can do, then the

[7] Ibid., 238.

condition that God has set for the fulfillment of His promise has been met. Can we fulfill our covenant responsibilities (by believing) and yet have God fail to fulfill His promise? It is not possible.

This is the historic Presbyterian view of children in the covenant.

> It is equally true, however, that if parents were unfaithful they had no right to expect any benefit whatever. There was no reason for satisfaction, or glorying in the name of the covenant, unless they observed the law of the covenant; unless they obeyed the will of God.[8]

But this unfaithfulness is not the same thing as "inadequate works." Every human parent has inadequate works. No human parent has met all the conditions of works that would ensure godly offspring. Godly children are not the result of our works. They are God's reward, God's covenant blessing. If God were to have my children turn out on the basis of my works—on one of my good days—they would all be in the penitentiary. But he offers to *give* me my children, and their children after them. What must I do? I must believe Him when He offers them to me.

Now if I believe Him, this faith is organically connected to parental faithfulness. But we are solid Protestants, and so we do not try to have the ox push the plow. Faith first and faith foundationally.

In this older view, believing God meant seeing faithful generations later. But in the modern American theology of children, we want to see first, then believe. We think that faith is the assurance of what we already have, the assurance of things highly visible. Before bringing a child into communion of the Church, we need more than God's promise. We need to hear from the child.

---

[8] Schenck, *Children in the Covenant*, 121.

Dr. Thornwell's arguments assumed that the indispensable condition of Church discipline was profession of faith. This Dr. Hodge reasoned was "perfectly intelligible and inevitable, if a personal and voluntary confession of faith is the indispensable condition of Church membership. If it is not, the principle is out of place. It does not belong to the theory of infant Church membership." Dr. Hodge himself believed that the child of Christian parents, no less than the adult who made a personal and voluntary profession of faith, was a member of the Church on the same basis of presumptive membership in the invisible Church. Consequently, he said, "we see not how this principle can be denied, in its application to the Church, without giving up our whole doctrine and abandoning the ground to the Independents and Anabaptists."[9]

This is quite true. If we believe God when He says that He made us one with our wives so that He could have godly offspring, then we should act as though we believe it. This means that we should teach our children to believe it. And this means, in its turn, that they should never know a time when they did not love and honor Jesus Christ, love His gospel, and love His Church. If we do anything else with our children, we are teaching them to doubt, not to believe.

Dr. Hodge heartily agreed with Dr. Bushnell in his teaching that the Christian character and life of the parent laid a scriptural foundation for expecting the children to be truly Christian, and that Christian nurture was the great means of their salvation. He objected, however, to the explanation which Dr. Bushnell gave of these facts . . . .Christian nurture was, then, the appointed, the natural, the normal, and ordinary means by which the children of believers were made truly children of God. Consequently it was the method which these leaders believed should be principally relied upon and employed for the salvation of their children. They recognized a marvelous

[9] Ibid., 99.

adaptation of this means to the end which it was intended to accomplish, and they were convinced that success was assured to them in its use by the covenant promise of God.[10]

We have to be careful in articulating this. Modern evangelicals have been taught to be highly suspicious of anyone who says that they have been a Christian "all their life." If we bring up our children as we are commanded, in the nurture and admonition of the Lord, they should not be able to remember a time when they were not Christians. But if we are sensitive to the concerns of many well-meaning evangelicals—who have seen more than one spiritual basket case who has "been a Christian his whole life"—we will teach our children to put it differently. Instead of saying, "I can't remember a time when I was not a Christian," they should say, "I can't remember a time when I did not love the Lord Jesus Christ." That is harder to argue with, and that is the result of covenant nurture. Further, it is the historic covenantal view of children.

> The principle of the Reformed faith, that the child brought up under Christian influence should never know a time when love to God was not an active principle in its life, was displaced by an assumption that even the offspring of the godly were born enemies of God and must await the crisis of conversion.[11]

We must return to the doctrine of covenantal succession. If we hold to infant baptism, we are saying by our participation in that wonderful rite that we believe God's promises concerning future generations. What this debate has shown is that more than a few paedobaptists are saying, "Really? You *believe* the promises? Isn't that works?"

[10] Ibid., 144–145.
[11] Ibid., 153.

23

Epilogue

A fitting way to conclude a book on the objectivity of the covenant would be by remembering two central points of application. The first concerns our attitude toward ourselves in what might be called the problem of the introspective conscience. The second concerns the unfortunate willingness many Christians have to pronounce on the regenerate status of others, in what might be dubbed the extrospective conscience.

We can begin by noting how Paul is introduced to us in the New Testament, "And [they] cast him out of the city, and stoned him: and the witnesses laid down their clothes at a young man's feet, whose name was Saul" (Acts 7:58). It has become commonplace in recent years for some scholars to minimize the "anguished conscience" aspect of Saul's conversion. This has appeared to them as an anachronistic projection of Luther's experience back into the first century. In this understanding, the apostle Paul's ministry was largely about bringing Jew and Gentile together in Christ, and less about God bringing God and man together in Christ. While believing this perspective to be mistaken on this point, it is important to note that the traditional take has developed some problems of its own. A similar point can be made with Abraham, although the evidence is not as pronounced. A traditional pietist cast of mind has resulted in equating godliness with an ongoing torment of soul. In contrast to this, the blessings of an objective covenant include the blessing of forgiveness and rest.

But it appears that as soon as we are stopped from rummaging around in our own hearts, we have an immediate yearning to rummage around in someone else's. We either doubt our own salvation with anguish or we doubt someone else's with satisfaction. An objective covenant deals with this also.

When God brings someone under conviction of sin, as He clearly did with Saul, the activity is teleological. That is, it is directed to a particular end, and when that end is achieved, the conviction and introspection cease. Saul is introduced to us at the stoning of Stephen (Acts 7:58), and this is done in a way that assumes his prior involvement in this situation. According to Jewish law, the witnesses against Stephen were to be the ones to throw the stones, but we know the witnesses were suborned (6:11) and set up to their false testimony (6:13). The men who put up the false witnesses were from a particular synagogue, and their number included men from Cilicia (6:9). Tarsus, Saul's hometown, was in Cilicia. These men were not able to handle Stephen in debate (6:10), and so they arranged for a judicial murder. Saul agreed with what happened to Stephen (8:1), and he emerges immediately as the leader in the subsequent savaging of the Church (8:3).

Clearly Saul did not just walk into a stoning in progress and join the mob. He was one of those who could not answer Stephen, and he was one of the those who arranged for the spurious testimony. But someone of Saul's genius would know that killing a man is not a refutation, and his losing to Stephen in public debate *had* to have rankled. Further, his frenzied persecution of the Church afterward seems to be a clear attempt to shout down an inner voice. We know that Saul was zealous for the law (Phil. 3:4–7), and we know from him what the law could do to such a man (Rom. 3:20; 5:20; 7:7–13). Saul's summary of his pre-Christian life was that it was dung (Phil. 3:8), and that he had been the chief of sinners (1 Tim. 1:15). He says that he had been an *insolent* man. His baptism was a washing away of his sins

(Acts 22:16), which were *many* and which he had come to see as wretched defilement. He cries out in Romans 7, "O *wretched* man . . ." But he also knows the point of such introspective yearning, which is forgiveness. "Who will *deliver* me?"

We see something similar with Abraham, although it is not as pronounced. Ur of the Chaldees was an idolatrous city. This means either that Abram was an idolater called to repentance or that he was a worshiper of the true God, reduced to the impotence of exile. We first meet Abram in Ur (Gen. 11:26) and Abram marries there, but in this condition of exile, Sarai his wife was barren (11:30). This fruitlessness is a type for sin, and Abram is called from this condition to be Abraham, in some sense the father of the world (Rom. 4:13).

The objectivity of the covenant is a true deliverance from morbid introspection. Those who want to come to the covenant without heart searching clearly do not understand the basics of the gospel. Abraham and Saul were wretched sinners, as were we all. But those who want to have their connection with the covenant be the point where they begin their morbid heart-searchings do not understand the gospel either. One of the central points of the new covenant is forgiveness of sin, and it is not too much to ask that forgiveness result in . . . *forgiveness*.

And when we get this lesson down, we become confident in our forgiveness and start doubting (with little evidence) the forgiveness of others. We have addressed this issue a number of times in this book, but to do so again is most necessary. We need to get this down. We are to take the baptisms of others at face value. We also take the teaching of Scripture at face value, and the behavior and words of these covenant members at face value. If there is conflict between what baptism means and what the baptized are openly doing and saying, then we are at liberty to point to the inconsistency and say that it constitutes covenantal faithlessness. But we need to be extremely wary of pronouncing on the secret things (Deut. 29:29). We have cited this verse a number of times in this book—it would be a good verse to memorize.

We should return, again and again, to the example of the faithful and faithless husband. To repeat the same things again and
again is a good thing (Phil. 3:1), especially when we are trying to
break a three-century-old bad habit.

To say that a man is a husband by covenant is not to say that he
is keeping the terms of it. Our inability to grasp this simple illustration (in either direction) should be a strong indicator that we
are in the grip of a powerful and erroneous idea. In this fallen
world, we have to grasp what happens whenever a covenant is
broken. When men and women marry, they exchange vows in
public, promising to forsake all others. Why is this necessary? The
answer is that we are a race of sinners, and we cannot assume that
people will do what they say they will. And so we exchange
vows, seeking to put the matter beyond dispute, as Paul in Hebrews tells us.

So again, when someone is baptized in the name of the Father,
Son and Holy Spirit, they are ushered into an objective, visible,
covenant membership. Regardless of the state of their heart, regardless of any hypocrisy, regardless of whether or not they mean
it, such a person is now a visible saint, a Christian. God has made
a statement concerning this person, and the one baptized has an
obligation to say *amen* to God's statement through how he goes on
to live his life.

A glance around at the baptized contemporary church shows
that many do not understand this. They contradict what God said
at their baptism through various heresies, immoralities, and com-
promises. This certainly does not unsettle the heavens—let God
be true and every man a liar—but it does create a problem. Unfortunately, the problem has not been addressed biblically by
those Christians who see the problem.

In the Church, we have covenant communion with one another. We have communion with the saints who have gone before
us to be with the Lord in heaven. We are all one, just as the loaf
broken in communion is one loaf. This is a great consolation, as it

should be, as we are seeking fellowship with other saints. But what are we to make of flagrant rebellion against God's Word from within the Church? Surely such rebels are not part of this communion, are they? What are we to make of the blemishes at our love feasts (Jude 12)? What are we to make of liberal bishops who deny the virgin birth and resurrection, or modern evangelicals who deny that God knows the future, or extreme charismatics who claim that God regularly adds to His Word through them?

I have argued in this book that to answer these questions, we must begin with understanding the reality of the objective covenant. Whenever someone is baptized, something really happens that puts them into communion with all other visible saints. This does not guarantee they will be faithful to that communion, but they must be a participant of the communion in order to be able to betray it. An American can betray his country, but a Canadian cannot betray the United States in the same way. A man who is married to a woman can betray her, but a man who never met her cannot do so.

We vary between two extremes. The first extreme is to say that people who are guilty of such things are not Christians at all, in any sense, and so we rid the body of Christ of them. Unfortunately, by doing this, we also have lost the very concept of a visible body of Christ. We find ourselves saying that a man who has never met Christ has betrayed Him. In other words, we say that all adulterers were never *really* married. But of course this means that they are not *really* adulterers.

The other extreme acknowledges that they are in fact Christians, and indeed, let the ecumenical games begin! But this is just as silly. This position is to maintain that if someone is a husband, then adultery is impossible, and we can only speak encouragingly to one another.

So when it comes to the "ecumenical question" we appear to be divided between two positions. The first is that we should accept all kinds of heretical "Christians" with all friendliness. The other is that we should reject their heresies, along with any title to the name *Christian*. In other words, we have two positions: the first is that husbands cannot commit adultery, and the second is that adulterers are not husbands, and hence not adulterers. What never seems to occur to anyone is the duty of fighting our fellow Christians to the last ditch—as Athanasius did with Arius.

When a husband has been chronically unfaithful to his wife, to say that he remains a husband is not to approve of his infidelity. It is the *basis* of the disapproval. Perhaps his wife should divorce him, but, until she does, he is a husband. No one would look at the pattern of his adulteries, and then say, "Oh, well, at least he is married." The fact that he is married compounds the sin, and in no way lessens it. In the same way, for an overt unbeliever to deny the deity of Jesus Christ is a great sin. But it is a *worse* sin for a baptized believer to do so, and for an ordained minister to reject the gospel in this way is far worse still. Such treachery should make us angrier; the fact that *additional* covenantal vows were broken ameliorates nothing.

Branches in Christ that bear much fruit are pruned and blessed. Do they have communion with those branches that bear no fruit, and which will be cut off and burned? They do not have a common future, but they do have a common present place on the same vine. To change the image slightly, together they partake of the root and fatness of the olive tree. And this means that true ecumenical dialogue with unfaithful Christians should consist of solemn warnings.

At the same time, we should see that our disapproval of fellow covenant members is an *objective* disapproval. We no longer disapprove because their "lack of regeneration" has been weighed in the balances of *our* discernment and been found wanting.

So the conclusion of the matter is here. First, the work of the law and a bad conscience are to bring us to Christ and His forgiveness. A man's conversion is to be the point where the introspective conscience ends, not the point where it *begins*. Consider the work of the introspective conscience to be like the pangs of child birth. It is *not* to be adopted as a way of life. And second, be wary of all temptations to manhandle the regeneration of other people. If covenant members are doing what is demonstrably wrong, and it is necessary for you to be involved, you may say that they are not being faithful to the covenant. And the response is to call them to faithfulness, call them to Christ, call them back to their baptism and to the terms of the covenant, and not to an invisible experience which neither you nor they would necessarily recognize.

Appendix:
The New Perspective on Paul

One of the stranger elements in the charge made by the RPCUS was that the heretical teachings that they condemned in us were inspired by what has come to be called the "New Perspective" on Paul. Many things were sloppily done in the presentation of these charges, but it has to be said that this one gets a blue ribbon at the fair.

First, what exactly is the "New Perspective" on Paul? Donald Hagner writes:

> Nearly twenty-five years ago E.P. Sanders published his book *Paul and Palestinian Judaism* and began what could well be called a Copernican revolution in Pauline studies. One of the leading advocates of the newer knowledge has dubbed it "The New Perspective on Paul." The revolution is far from complete. Some of us, moreover, continue to believe that the evidence still points to a geocentric universe—at least so far as Paul's theology is concerned.[1]

The man who named this movement was James Dunn—but N.T. Wright is a well-known (and fairly conservative) exponent of the perspective. While there are many insights of great value in this movement, particularly from Wright, I have to say that the foundational tenets of the New Perspective are off-base.

[1] Peter Stuhlmacher, *Revisiting Paul's Doctrine of Justification: A Challenge to the New Perspective* (Downers Grove, Ill.: InterVarsity Press, 2001), 75–76.

Those things of value that can be found there are not unique to
the movement, and those things which distinguish the school of
thought are erroneous.[2]

The basic tenets of the movement are, first, that the Judaism
of the first century was not a "works religion." Acceptance before
God was not earned through a merit system of righteousness
based on works. Secondly, it is held that justification by faith does
not represent the center of Pauline theology. Rather, Paul argued
for justification as a pragmatic tactic as he sought to advance his
mission to the Gentiles. In this view, Paul's passion was the union
of Jew and Gentile together in the Church, without such "bound-
ary markers" as circumcision, and that arguments for justification
by faith were simply employed because they advanced that cause.

It is also common to say that Paul's theology (as it actually was)
has been misunderstood by us because it has been read through
the lens of Martin Luther's great crisis of conscience, as Krister
Stendahl argued.[3] They want to maintain that Paul was actually
addressing a particular problem at a particular time (which problem was that of getting Jews and Gentiles together), and that his
gospel does not address the universal human dilemma—at least
not in the way that we have readily assumed. It is too often
thought, so the argument goes, that the medieval merit theology
of Rome is glibly wrapped around the necks of first-century rab-
bis. Augustine saw his own tormented experience in Paul's, and
so has the Western world ever since. Martin Luther saw his own
tormented experience in Paul's, and so has the Protestant world
ever since.

But while psychological details of conversion must vary, there
is a constant human problem with self-righteousness. Luther saw
a universal gospel that solved the universal and powerful

[2] At the same time, I agree with Rich Lusk's exhortation to give Wright a
sympathetic hearing. *Reformation and Revival Journal* 11, no. 2 (spring 2002):
35.

[3] Krister Stendahl, *Paul Among Jews and Gentiles* (Philadelphia: Fortress Press,
1976), 78–96.

human urge to justify itself before God. In this, it has to be said that Luther was pastorally astute, and the New Perspective adherents tend to be pastorally naive. Sanders, one New Perspective theologian, makes a great distinction between works to enter the covenant and works to maintain one's status in the covenant. But anyone who has ever counseled troubled souls understands that this is a distinction without a practical pastoral difference. A wink is as good as a nod to a blind horse. Thinking that my salvation depends upon my works to *keep* it is the same error as thinking it depends on my works to *get* it. Having begun by the Spirit, what makes us think we can finish in the flesh?

At least some of the attractiveness of the New Perspective appears to be a reaction to the Holocaust—which maintains that any charge against Judaism was assumed to be a hair's breadth away from anti-Semitism. Hence it was important to say that first-century Judaism was a religion of *grace* because to maintain otherwise was to be critical of the Jews. But there is a difference between criticizing the self-righteousness of Judaism (which the New Testament requires of us) and murdering Jews (which the New Testament forbids).

The problem with this aspect of the New Perspective is that it collides with the data.

> Thou blind Pharisee, cleanse first that which is within the cup and platter, that the outside of them may be clean also. (Mt. 23:26)

> And the Lord said unto him, Now do ye Pharisees make clean the outside of the cup and the platter; but your inward part is full of ravening and wickedness. (Lk. 11:39)

> The Pharisee stood and prayed thus with himself, God, I thank thee, that I am not as other men are, extortioners, unjust, adulterers, or even as this publican. I fast twice in the week, I give tithes of all that I possess. (Lk. 18:11–12).

Though I might also have confidence in the flesh. If any other man thinketh that he hath whereof he might trust in the flesh, I more: Circumcised the eighth day, of the stock of Israel, of the tribe of Benjamin, an Hebrew of the Hebrews; as touching the law, a Pharisee. (Phil. 3:4–5)

But if ye had known what this meaneth, I will have mercy, and not sacrifice, ye would not have condemned the guiltless. (Mt. 12:7)

Ye hypocrites, well did Esaias prophesy of you, saying, This people draweth nigh unto me with their mouth, and honoureth me with their lips; but their heart is far from me. (Mt. 15:7–8)

For they being ignorant of God's righteousness, and going about to establish their own righteousness, have not submitted themselves unto the righteousness of God. (Rom. 10:3)

If the average Bible-reading Christian takes a dim view of first-century Judaism, it is evident where he got that dim view. Read through the New Testament, and simply mark every polemical comment directed at the Pharisees, Sadducees, the circumcision, the Jews, and so on. The evidence is so clear that it takes about three years of graduate work in theological studies, on average, to erase it.[4]

It is therefore not at all evident, in my opinion, that there were no Jews around in the time of Paul who corresponded to the legalists attacked by him in the traditional understanding of works-righteousness. I am reminded of the wry remark of C.K. Barrett: "He is a bold man who supposes that he understands first-century Judaism better than Paul did."[5]

[4] And as if to underline the point further, Christ destroyed Jerusalem in A.D. 70. In doing this, He made the judicial declaration that their collective, national self-righteousness was horrendous. Jerusalem suffered the same fate as Sodom, which shows they had rejected *God's* grace in Christ.

[5] Stuhlmacher, 88.

The tendency to justify oneself is universal, and all of us can see it on a daily basis. This tendency, this way of all flesh, does not disappear when men become religious; rather, it is accentuated. The only effective antidote to it is sovereign grace, high-octane Calvinistic grace. When the cross is preached effectively and justification by faith alone is insisted upon, this throws down man's innate tendency to preen himself. Nothing else does this. Paul knew it, Augustine knew it, Luther knew it, Calvin knew it.

With regard to the second point that justification was really a peripheral concern to Paul, J. Gresham Machen deserves a hearing.

> The real reason why Paul was devoted to the doctrine of justification by faith was not that it made possible the Gentile mission, but rather that it was true. Paul was not devoted to the doctrine of justification by faith because of the Gentile mission; he was devoted to the Gentile mission because of the doctrine of justification by faith.[6]

As the other chapters in this book testify, I do take exception with Martin Luther at a number of important points, the relation of law and grace being one of them. At the same time, on this question of a man's standing before God through faith, Stephen Westerholm's comment is appropriate: "Students who want to understand Paul but feel they have nothing to learn from Martin Luther should consider a career in metallurgy."[7]

The New Perspective is right in emphasizing that there is a corporate aspect to justification. But this is a position that can be held without contradiction by a critic of the New Perspective.[8] Individual justification is not the only kind of justification there is, as was argued in an earlier chapter.

---

[6] J. Gresham Machen, *The Origin of Paul's Religion* (London: Hodder & Stoughton, 1921), 278–279.

[7] Stuhlmacher, 93.

[8] Ibid., 16–17.

In short, the New Perspective tends to present us with a false dilemma, either "Lutheran" individual justification or corporate justification, where God is making one new man out of Jew and Gentile. But there is no reason why we should agree to a dilemma that forces us to choose between eggs and omelettes. It is possible to have both, as the rest of this book has been seeking to show.

Bibliography

Avis, Paul. *The Church in the Theology of the Reformers*. London: Marshall Morgan & Scott, 1981.

Booth, Randy. "Covenantal Antithesis." In *The Standard Bearer: A Festschrift for Greg Bahnsen*, ed. by Steve Schlissel, 29–64. Nagadoches, Tex.: Covenant Media Press, 2002.

Calvin, John. *Calvin's Commentaries*. Grand Rapids: Baker, 1979.

Frame, John. "Law and Gospel." <http://www.chalcedon.edu/articles/0201/020104frame.shtml>.

Garver, S. Joel. "Scriptural Indications." In *Taking Apostasy Seriously* [online collection of essays]. <http://www.lasalle.edu/~garver/apostasy.htm>.

———. "Reformed Dogmatics." In *Taking Apostasy Seriously* [online collection of essays].<http://www.lasalle.edu/~garver/apostasy.htm>.

———. "John Calvin on Apostasy." In *Taking Apostasy Seriously* [online collection of essays].<http://www.lasalle.edu/~garver/apostasy.htm>.

———. "A Brief Catechesis on Covenant and Baptism." <http://www.lasalle.edu/~garver/cateches.htm>.

Knox, Ronald. *The Quotable Knox*. San Francisco: Ignatius Press, 1996.

Leithart, Peter. "'Framing' Sacramental Theology: Trinity and Symbol." *Westminster Theological Journal* 62 (2000).

———. "Modernity and the 'Merely Social.'" *Pro Ecclesia* 9, no. 3.

———. "Womb of the World: Baptism and Priesthood of the New Covenant in Hebrews 10:19–22." *Journal for the Study of the New Testament* 78 (June 2000).

————. "Conjugating the Rites: Old and New in Augustine's Theory of Signs." *Calvin Theological Journal* 34 (1999).

————. "'Judge Me, O God': Biblical Perspectives on Justification." <http://www.hornes.org/theologia/content/peter_leithart/judge_me_o_god_biblical_perspectives_on_justification.htm>.

Lusk, Rich. "N.T. Wright and Reformed Theology:Friend or Foes?" *Reformation and Revival Journal* Vol. 11, No. 2 (spring 2002).

Machen, J. Gresham. *The Origin of Paul's Religion*. London: Hodder & Stoughton, 1921.

Mathison, Keith. *The Shape of Sola Scriptura*. Moscow, Idaho: Canon Press, 2001.

Nevin, John Williamson. *The Mystical Presence*. Eugene, OR: Wipf and Stock, 2000 [1846].

Newton, John. *The Works of John Newton*. Carlisle, Penn.: Banner of Truth, 1985 [1820].

Seraiah, Chori. "The God of Contingencies." <http://www.cmfnow.com/RPCUS/seraiah.html>.

Schenck, Lewis. *The Presbyterian Doctrine of Children in the Covenant*. New Haven:Yale UP, 1940.

Stendahl, Krister. *Paul Among Jews and Gentiles*. Philadelphia: Fortress Press, 1976.

Strange, Alan. "Sacraments, The Spirit, and Human Inability." *Mid-American Journal of Theology* 12 (2001).

Stuhlmacher, Peter. *Revisiting Paul's Doctrine of Justification: A Challenge to the New Perspective*. Downers Grove, Ill.: InterVarsity Press, 2001.

Wallace, Ronald. *Calvin's Doctrine of the Word and Sacrament*. Eugene, Ore.:Wipf and Stock, 1982.

Warfield, B.B. *The Plan of Salvation*. Boonton, N.J.: Simpson Publishing Co., 1989.

Wilson, Douglas. *Standing on the Promises*. Moscow, Idaho: Canon Press, 1997.